THE SOUTH DOWNS WAY

The Irreverent Guide to Walking and Cycling . . .

THE
SOUTH DOWNS
WAY

Martin King

MAINSTREAM
PUBLISHING

EDINBURGH AND LONDON

First published in Great Britain in 2002 by
MAINSTREAM PUBLISHING COMPANY (EDINBURGH) LTD
7 Albany Street
Edinburgh EH1 3UG

ISBN 1 84018 411 6

A catalogue record for this book is available from the British Library

Typeset in Futurist and Garamond
Printed and bound in Great Britain by
Cox & Wyman Ltd

CONTENTS

PART ONE

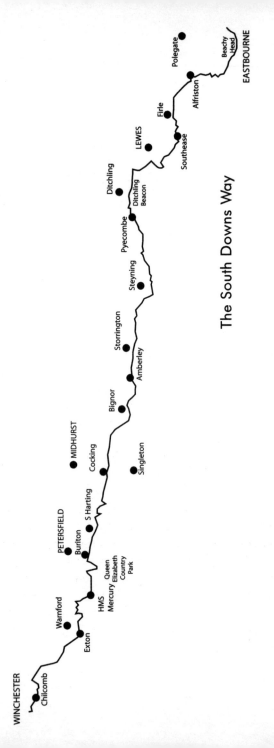

The South Downs Way

The Way Ahead

THE SOUTH DOWNS WAY is a 100-mile-long national trail that runs from Eastbourne in East Sussex to Winchester in Hampshire. The route is Britain's first long-distance bridleway. This scenic and picturesque trail runs across the open, rambling expanse of the Sussex Downs. At the top of the Downs you sometimes feel that you could fly; the views of villages and towns down below on a clear day are unbelievable. One minute you might be climbing up a hill with a panoramic view out to sea on one side and on the other a vista of the rolling green fields of the English countryside, and for the next few miles you might pass through woods and by fast-running rivers. The terrain is constantly changing, but that is the beauty of the South Downs Way. It is estimated that over one million people a year visit the South Downs, and no wonder, with so much to see.

The South Downs Way is steeped in history, with iron-age forts, Roman villas and roads, Saxon and Norman churches and castles, medieval towns and villages, and an abundance of wildlife and plant life. There are sheep grazing high on ridges which stretch for miles. Bird and butterfly watchers are in heaven up on the South Downs – it's every twitcher's paradise. Along the Way there are many National Trust properties and places of interest, and there are also the seaside towns of Eastbourne, Brighton, Worthing, Littlehampton and Bognor Regis. Towards the city of Chichester there are some good views from the Downs of Hayling Island, and the city of Portsmouth and its naval history, and out towards the Solent and the chalk hills and cliffs of the Isle of Wight.

Every step of the way there is something new around the corner, whether you're walking, cycling or on horseback. Whether you're up on the Downs for a short leisurely stroll, out biking for the day, attempting to do the whole route or out with the family having a picnic, the sights and sounds, colours and smells will make you want to come back for another trip.

I had heard about the South Downs Way from a friend of mine who, like me, was a black-cab driver in London. He had cycled it from Winchester to Eastbourne and was also a regular on the annual London–Brighton cycle ride. He was a bit of an oddball – exercise and black cabbies don't really mix. A few years later I was out with some friends when one of them, Keith, got around to talking about cycling the South Downs Way. Keith, who is a plumber by trade, is loud and does everything at 100mph. He again aroused my interest in the South Downs Way and the challenge of completing such a distance on a bike when he told me that he and two others had cycled the Way in its entirety twice before, and that one of his mates, a doctor, had cycled the whole route in one day.

From then on I was interested – it seemed like a challenge – and after months of talking about it the boys asked me to do it with them. That was it. Next day I was out on the bike training, nothing too drastic at first, just about a mile, to the paper shop and back, but a date was set for the ride. The most-asked questions were: Would I make it? Had I trained to cycle over 100 miles? Was I taking the whole thing far too lightly? Just to show I could do it, and do it comfortably, I told the doubting Thomases that I would not only cycle it in two days but would also walk it from Winchester to Eastbourne, the opposite to the way we were going to cycle, and that is what I did. On my travels I documented both the cycle and the walk, giving information for both the walker and the cyclist: where to stop for a break, refreshments, pubs, hotels, bike-repair shops, tourist information, taxis, buses, trains, phone numbers, tips on what to take on your journey and what to wear. This is a step-by-step alternative guide by someone who has actually walked and cycled the South Downs Way – how many authors of similar books can say that?

The Pleasure of the Downs

THE SOUTH DOWNS WAY runs from Eastbourne in East Sussex to the city of Winchester in Hampshire. The 100-mile-long ancient route passes through some of Southern England's most scenic countryside. The trail was Britain's first long-distance bridleway, and is accessible to a wide range of people. With over one million visitors every year estimated to enjoy the pleasures of the South Downs Way, you can see why such a vast cross-section of people spend time here – disabled people (parts of the walk are accessible by wheelchair), mountain bikers, horse riders, walkers, picnickers, paragliders, kite flyers, bird watchers, fishermen and geologists to name but a few.

With most sections of the way having car-parking facilities, there are panoramic views and beautiful countryside to discover. One minute you may be high up on the ridge of the Downs and the next crossing a stream, strolling through a picturesque village or cutting through a deep valley or woods. The scenery continually changes. The vast open spaces and lack of traffic noise give a great sense of tranquillity and quiet isolation. Along the South Downs Way there are some delightful villages and towns and most have a pub or restaurant, or a tea-room or café. There is always somewhere to stop for refreshments.

The Way is signposted by a distinctive acorn symbol, making it easy to follow the trail. It runs mostly over chalk so the surface is reasonably firm and dry all year round. The South Downs Way is maintained by the local authorities, with financial support from the Countryside Commission. Guided walks and cycle rides are available in East and West Sussex, and there are plenty of hotels, guesthouses, youth hostels and bed and breakfast facilities along the whole stretch of the Way. Also there are caravan, campsites and tourist information offices. In fact, there is something for everyone. If you're just giving the dog a quick run, or walking or cycling the whole length of the trail, you are sure to enjoy the beauty of the South Downs Way.

Getting there is easy. Trains run regularly from London to Winchester, Petersfield, Amberley, Glynde, Berwick, Lewes or Eastbourne stations, and by car it is just over an hour and a half's drive from central London. From the coast, you are never more than a short drive or leisurely cycle away from the South Downs. There is also a good network of short walks and cycle routes that give you the opportunity to discover places in and around the South Downs Way.

The History of the Way

DURING THE STONE AGE nomadic peoples wandered the Downs and the coastal areas hunting deer, wild boar, birds and fish. The climate changed dramatically during the Ice Age. The ice never spread over the Downs, but when it melted elsewhere forests grew and the nomadic population of the Middle Stone Age increased. Some 5,000 years ago, these new tribes crossed the narrow sea from the continent and settled on the Downs. The new settlers were far more sophisticated than the inhabitants of the Downs and brought with them pottery, flint agriculture and farming. They kept domestic animals, and cleared whole areas of shrubs and trees, becoming the first group of people to grow crops in Britain. Even today, parts of the landscape have changed little since the shift from a hunter-gatherer culture to a more sophisticated community that settled in one place.

Neolithic times saw the landscape change yet again, with large enclosures or meeting places, ceremonial compounds and communal graves constructed high up on the Downs. Some of these graves are up to 200ft long, where whole families or clans were buried.

The Bronze Age came, and with it single burial mounds of which hundreds can still be seen today. They are marked on maps as *tumuli* and are mostly found on the high points along the Way, which during Bronze Age times was a busy trading route. The Bronze Age economy was based on farming, with the cross dykes found on today's landscapes being boundaries, and stock pens and enclosures.

Celtic settlers around 650 BC are believed to be responsible for the first use of iron and more changes in how people lived and farmed occurred. Yet again more woodlands were cleared and the population grew; fields were used for crops and farmsteads were set up. The new sharp iron tools enabled Iron Age people to build camps and hill forts. These defensive positions were a product of squabbling and inter-tribal rivalry. Old Winchester Hill, Chanctonbury and Cissbury Ring are all fine examples.

The next big changes came with the Romans, who built roads from Chichester and Lewes to London. These routes were ideal for transporting iron, corn and troops. One road, Stane Street, can still be seen along with a Roman villa at nearby Bignor. So the South Downs Way was connected to the various routes, across the downlands, through hamlets and villages and down to the coast.

The Saxons arrived by ship and made their way inland, conquering and colonising. They were more interested in the rich, unspoilt soil of the downland fields and valleys than they were in the high downs, which had been cultivated for over 2,000 years by then. Each township they formed included pastures for pigs, cattle and sheep as well as arable land for crops.

The Norman conquest of 1066 through to the Black Death of the 1340s was a period of population growth for the South Downs. New market towns sprang up, coastal ports were busy and trade from abroad was on the increase. The church owned large estates and although Christianity was slow to be accepted in the south of England, before long nearly every village had its own church, built using local stone and materials.

By the 14th century the population of the South Downs was dwindling fast. The plague wiped out whole villages, such as Exceat, and places like Bramber, Botolphs, Edburton and Coombes shrank considerably in size. Chalk quarrying came to be one of the main industries, and by the 18th century Amberley, Sullington, Beeding, Clayton and Beddingham all had working chalk pits. The surrounding rivers were improved and a period of canal building took place, so that the chalk and lime could be transported to various places across the south. This period also saw the growth of the coastal resorts, and places which were once no more than fishing ports boomed almost overnight. With road improvements and sea bathing becoming fashionable, there was an increase in visitors.

During the Napoleonic Wars troops were stationed along the coast. The many high vantage points along the Downs were soon filled with lookout posts and military garrisons. The seaside towns expanded and a rich social life attracted even more incomers. Royal patronage saw an influx of visitors; Brighton, Bognor Regis, Worthing, Littlehampton and Eastbourne were all visited by royalty and the crowds flocked to bathe in the grey waters of the English Channel. In 1750, Dr Richard Russell published a dissertation extolling the benefits of sea bathing. In it he claimed that sea bathing was an excellent treatment for glandular diseases and the town then earned its nickname of 'Dr Brighton'.

In 1841 the railway paved the way for thousands of people to visit the coast on cheap day excursions. Many people lived less than 50 miles away in London and the suburbs, but had never seen the sea. The 19th century saw the arrival of cheap food from the Commonwealth and Australasia. Many farmers now found planting the Downs with crops unprofitable and turned the land over to sheep farming.

Some envisaged profit in selling land to property developers and the area experienced a boom in housing.

Local individuals, charities and some area authorities between 1900 and 1945 bought land that they saw as being under threat from over-development; the area between Beachy Head and Seaford was one such stretch. The Town and Country Planning Act of 1947 brought indiscriminate and speculative house building under control. Since then the whole of the South Downs Way has been protected, sections of it being under the control of a number of national and local trusts. Much of the scarp and hillside is sites of scientific interest, many buildings are listed and undamaged archaeological sites are now ancient monuments. As a result of all these conservation measures the South Downs is still an area of outstanding natural beauty, and today's visitor will see little change from how the area looked during the Stone, Iron and Bronze Ages, and Roman, Saxon and Norman times.

The Way has a good mixture of rolling hills, cornfields, shrub and grassland, woods and forests, streams and rivers, beaches and cliffs, ridge-top walks and panoramic views. There is something for everyone, so get out there and enjoy it.

Downland Wildlife

IN RECENT YEARS THE South Downs has been declared an environmentally sensitive area and local farmers have been encouraged by financial aid in the form of grants to move back to more traditional methods of farming, which means fewer or no fertilisers or pesticides. Sheep grazing keeps the grass in some areas to a manageable level and this is where plants and other wildlife flourish. During the summer, you will find many wild herbs and plants with strange names such as squinancywort, hoary stock, salad burnet, round-headed rampion, scabious and autumn lady's tresses, along with many types of orchids such as the purple and the common spotted types – also look out for burnt, fragrant, pyramidal, frog, musk, bee and green-winged varieties.

There is varied wildlife with rare snails, beetles, grasshoppers and many different types of moths and butterflies, hedgehogs, mice, rats, weasels, stoats and polecats. You are sure to see plenty of sheep, rabbits, hares and cows, and the odd fallow deer, badger and fox. You may even come across llamas, and keep a lookout for ostriches and pumas. The bird life up on the Way is an ornithologist's paradise. On the high ridges you may see buzzards and kestrels floating on the thermals, sparrows, robins on fence posts posing for Christmas cards, wheatears, skylarks, swallows and swifts, house-martins, woodpeckers, magpies, jays, wood pigeons and tawny owls. Down near the streams and rivers you may find kingfishers, moorhens, mallards, pied wagtails and herons, and along the coastal stretches look out for gulls, jackdaws, pipits, redshanks and oystercatchers. On the shoreline between the Seven Sisters Country Park and Eastbourne there's a good chance you may see a common or grey seal. These mammals come ashore to breed and are becoming more frequently seen.

Practical Advice

THE MOST IMPORTANT RULE in the summer months up on the South Downs is 'keep it light'; if you're walking or cycling don't carry things you don't need – it's as simple as that. If you're walking, wear a pair of good, comfortable, waterproof walking boots and thick socks; don't try and break in new boots on a long walk. Trainers can lead to blisters and they are not really suitable footwear over a long distance, particularly since some of the track is quite stony and uneven. Wear loose-fitting clothing for comfort. Shorts and a T-shirt should be fine if the weather allows. Remember that in the summer months the South Downs can get very hot, so pack some sun cream and wear a baseball cap or sun hat to protect your head.

If you suffer from hay fever make sure you have some medication with you, as on some stretches there are fields of fresh-cut corn and hay which will get your nose twitching and your eyes streaming and make your throat dry. Pack a first-aid kit with some plasters and Vaseline. All parts of your body can get sore, and I mean all parts, so go well prepared – there are gorse and stinging nettles in some places, which you can unknowingly brush past, so pack an anti-histamine cream. It will also come in handy for bee and wasp stings. Carry a set of lightweight waterproof trousers and a jacket. You never know when you might need them, for the weather can change very quickly. Cyclists should wear a safety helmet, carry a repair kit and a spare inner tube, some spanners or a small tool kit, and have lights.

You may need sunglasses, and you should pack a rucksack with plenty of water or an energy drink, or both, a sandwich and a snack like a Mars Bar and some fruit. You will want to treasure your memories of this glorious piece of English countryside so remember to take a camera with a film. Bring some emergency loo paper too, because you never know when you could get caught short!

Always carry a map and/or guidebook. A watch comes in very handy and a mobile phone could be a lifesaver, but make sure that it's charged up before you set off, and that you have some credit on it if it's a pay-as-you-go. On most mobile networks you can get a signal nearly the whole length of the Way. Always carry a torch, a compass and a whistle; it may get dark sooner then you expect, and misty or foggy along the coastal stretches. Plan your journey in advance, and tell people of your plans. If you do happen to get lost, don't panic – study your map, get your bearings, take your time, and if need be retrace your steps. You'll soon be back on the right path. Most of the Way is well signposted by the distinctive acorn symbol. On the whole walkers tend to be very polite and approachable, so if you need some assistance don't be afraid to ask.

If you plan to stay at a hotel or youth hostel remember to book well in advance. If you're camping, there are a number of campsites on the Way, but remember to ask before you pitch your tent in a farmer's field. Most will give permission if you're polite. Always keep your dogs on a lead or under close control and follow the country code.

Try not to drink alcohol when walking – don't go for a pub lunch and consume large amounts of booze or you may find you soon become dehydrated and suffer from stomach cramps. You will feel very uncomfortable when you try to get up and down some of the steep hills on the Way. In winter wrap up well and take a flask of hot tea or soup. If you're setting off in the morning, have a substantial breakfast before you leave.

Useful Information

RAIL

There are regular services to the major towns at both the start and finish of the Way. From London's Victoria station you can get the Eastbourne train and, if you wish, alight at either Lewes, Glynde, Berwick or Polgate, or travel from Victoria to Brighton and pick up a local train for Falmer, Shoreham, Plumpton or Cooksbridge. From Waterloo or Victoria you can take a train to Amberley, Arundel, Worthing or Chichester. Trains also run from Waterloo to Petersfield and Winchester. You can take cycles on the trains, and a timetable is available from all of the above stations.

BUS

A free public transport map and timetables are available from the East Sussex Highways and Transportation Dept, Sackville House, Brooks Close, Lewes BN7 1UE, or phone the county bus line on 01273 474747.

CAR

You can pick up the start/finish at Winchester on the M3 and the Way runs through or near these major roads heading out towards Eastbourne: A272, A31, A32, A27, A259, A286, A285, A29, A24, M23 and A22. There are lots of car parks along the whole stretch, many with panoramic views.

TOURIST INFORMATION
All of the tourist information centres listed below will help
you find places to stay in and around the South Downs Way.

Pevensey Tel: 01323 761444
Eastbourne Tel: 01323 411400
Seaford Tel: 01323 897426
Lewes Tel: 01273 483448
Brighton Tel: 01273 323755
Hove Tel: 01273 746100
Hove Town Hall Tel: 01273 778087
Shoreham Tel: 01273 452086
Worthing Tel: 01903 210022
Fontwell A27 Tel: 01243 543269
Bognor Regis Tel: 01243 823140
Chichester Tel: 01243 775888
Petersfield Tel: 01730 68829
Winchester Tel: 01962 840500

YOUTH HOSTELS
Beachy Head Tel: 01323 721081
Alfriston Tel: 01323 870423
Telescombe Tel: 01273 301357
Patcham Tel: 01273 556196
Truleigh Hill Tel: 01903 813419
Arundel Tel: 01903 882204
Winchester Tel: 01962 853723

CAMPING
For a list of farms where you can camp, send £1.50 to:

The Sussex Downs Conservation Board, Chanctonbury
House, Church Street, Storrington, West Sussex RH20 4LT.

GUIDED WALKS

For a booklet on guided walks and cycle rides, write to:

The Countryside Management Service, Southover House, Southover Road, Lewes, East Sussex, BN7 1YA

or:

The County Secretary, West Sussex County Council, County Hall, Chichester

Or contact the South Downs Rangers for advice and information. Tel: 01903 741234

HORSE RIDERS

Here is a list of saddlers along or near the Downs:

Leonard Stevens, 16 Crown Street, Eastbourne
Tel: 01323 734496
Polegate Saddlery, 3 Millfield, Station Road, Polegate
Tel: 01323 483382
Dragonfly Saddlery, Ditchling Crossroads, Ditchling
Tel: 01273 844606
Brendon Horse Centre, London Road, Pyecombe
Tel: 01273 844508
The Hove Tackroom, 424/426 Portland Road, Hove
Tel: 01273 410200
Equitogs, Country Garden Centre, Littlehampton Road, Worthing
Tel: 01903 507266
Geoff Dean, London Road, Ashington
Tel: 01903 892002
Petersfield Saddlery, Lyndum House, High Street
Tel: 01730 66816

FARRIERS

Here is a list of farriers on or near the South Downs:

John Henty, The Steel Works, Lower Road, Eastbourne
    Tel: 01323 721938
T. Goswell, 65 Broad Road, Lower Willingdon, Eastbourne
    Tel: 01323 488198
David Kneller, 28 Queensway, Seaford
    Tel: 01323 892988
Tony Phillips, 3 Chartwell Close, Beacon Heights, Seaford
    Tel: 01323 890242
Graham Baker, Glynde Forge, Glynde
    Tel: 01273 858474
Frank and Roger Dean, The Forge Mill Lane, Rodmell
    Tel: 01273 474740
William Weeding, Forge Cottage, Ringmer
    Tel: 01273 813024
Richard Chard, 1 Hayleigh Farm Cottages, Streat Lane, Streat
    Tel: 01273 891033
Alan Clarke, 2a Barn Close, Albourne, Hassocks
    Tel: 01273 832957
Kevin White, 20 Furzeland Way, Sayers Common, Hassocks
    Tel: 01273 834225
James Pimm, The Forge, Lower Beeding
    Tel: 01403 891686
P. L. Barnett, The Forge Kings, Barn Lane, Steyning
    Tel: 01903 816324
Christopher Peacock, 1 Charlton Court Cottages, Mouse
    Lane, Steyning Tel: 01903 813445
Stephen Jefford, 6 Malthouse Close, Arundel
    Tel: 01903 883676
Peter Fenton, Club Cottage, Top Road, Slindon
    Tel: 01243 814492

David Froggat, The Forge, West Dean, Chichester
Tel: 01243 811701

David Lewis, Fryern Home Farm, Fryern Park, Storrington
Tel: 01903 740159

Henry Alston, 1 Greenfields, Sutton, Pulborough
Tel: 01798 869302

Sidney Smith, 15 Mant Road, Petworth
Tel: 01798 342330

John Behan, 18 Guillods Cottages, Graffham
Tel: 01798 867265

Mark Broadbridge, Norwood Equestrian Centre, Norwood
Lane, Graffham Tel: 01798 867612

Robert Loxwood, Forge Cottage, Church Hill, Midhurst
Tel: 01730 813208

Colin White, Great Todham Farm House, Ambersham,
Midhurst Tel: 01730 816819

Donald Wilkinson, The Forge, Funtington, Chichester
Tel: 01243 577755

Richard Moss, The Forge, Froxfield Green, Petersfield
Tel: 01730 263536

Richard Lovejoy, 2 Chalkdell Cottages, East Meon
Tel: 01730 823646

Alan and David Povey, The Forge, Owslesbury, Winchester
Tel: 01962 777473

Bernard Malone, 23 Shepherds Road, Winchester
Tel: 01962 862662

VETS

If, while out on the Way, your dog or horse gets injured or becomes ill, a vet may be necessary. For a more comprehensive list check your local *Yellow Pages*.

St Anne's veterinary group, 6 St Anne's Road, Eastbourne
    Tel: 01323 640011

The Cliffe veterinary group, Radstock House, 21 High Street,
    Lewes Tel: 01273 473232

The Cliffe veterinary group, 57 Warren Way, Woodingdean,
    Brighton Tel: 01273 302609

Crossways veterinary group, The Paddocks, Furner's Lane,
    Henfield Tel: 01273 495227

Crossways veterinary group, 2 High Street, Steyning
    Tel: 01903 816428

The Surgery, 43a School Hill, Storrington
    Tel: 01903 743040

Ashton and Parners, The Equine Veterinary Hospital, Upper
    Tortington, Arundel Tel: 01903 883050

Arun veterinary group, 121 Lower Street, Pulborough
    Tel: 01798 872089

Downland veterinary group, 2 Stirling Road, Chichester
    Tel: 01243 786101

Walmsley and partners, Equine Veterinary Hospital, Home
    Park, Petersfield Tel: 01428 723594

Watson and Kennedy, Stable Close veterinary clinic, St Cross
    Road, Winchester Tel: 01962 840505

PART TWO

The Cycle – Day One

EASTBOURNE–BRAMBER

IT'S THE MORNING OF the ride. I finished work at 2 a.m. but set my alarm clock for 5.30 that morning. Tired but excited, I make myself get up. The boys are picking me up at 6 and then we're planning on having a fried breakfast in a café near Shoreham. A mate of mine recommended it, but we didn't plan on Nigel not being able to get his arse out of bed before we finally set off about 7, in Keith's van. We head off to the start of the South Downs Way, on the outskirts of Eastbourne.

Keith's son Daniel is dropping us off. We strap the four bikes onto the back of the van. Me, Keith and Gary sit on the floor in the back. Keith has cleared the van of all his plumbing tools and fittings and laid out a nice, clean, white dustsheet for us all to sit on, though after ten minutes my bum's gone numb. Nigel sits in the front with Daniel. We explain to him where the café is in Shoreham, and he tells us not to worry, he knows the place and will tell Daniel where to turn off.

Off we go. The three of us are chatting away in the back and Nigel and Daniel talk away in the front. Next thing one of us sits up and looks out the window and we've gone about ten miles past our turn-off for the café. We all look at one another.

'Nigel, you're meant to be watching out for the turn-off.'
'I am,' he replied.
'Then why the fuck have we gone ten miles past it?'

Keith, the diplomatic one of the four of us, says not to worry, there's bound to be somewhere in Eastbourne to get some grub. We arrive in Eastbourne and, after a half-hour drive around, stop and have breakfast in a grotty café in the town centre. It's like something out of a '60s black-and-white TV series – you can imagine Roger Moore as Simon Templar in *The Saint* sitting in here on the red plastic leatherette seats, sipping frothy coffee from a glass cup (before it became trendy and the name changed to 'cappuccino'), listening to a group of beatnik men in smocks with little Jimmy Hill beards passing a joint around and playing the bongos while reciting poetry. This place must have been cool in the hip late '50s and early '60s, and the sausage, egg and bacon on my plate looks like it has come from that era too – it is fucking awful, hard, cold and burnt. After abusing our stomachs we stock up with Lucozade and Mars Bars from the shop next door, then set off in the van to find the start of the South Downs Way.

Keith has ridden the South Downs Way in this direction twice before, but he can't quite remember where it started, the fucking plank. We drive around for nearly an hour, but for the life of us we can't find it.

'Come on Keith, think,' we all plead.

'I know it's near a school,' is all he can say, rubbing his head with his fingers as if to try and stimulate his memory.

Meanwhile Nigel is sitting in the front giving Daniel instructions from the map he has on his lap: 'Left here, right there, left here, turn here, stop here.' Round and round we go until Keith recognises a school. 'We're very close,' he says.

'I fucking hope so,' Gary and I tune in. 'We've been going round in circles for an hour.'

Keith takes the map from Nigel, who in the past hour has more than proved he is incapable of reading it.

'Right, Daniel,' says Keith. 'Take a left here, right here and stop. Gentleman, we are here.' He smiles, relieved we've made it at last.

We clamber from the back of the van. It feels good to stretch my legs. The sun is breaking through the clouds and I wonder how I will fare on such a long ride.

We untie the bikes from the rear of the van and check we have all our bags with everything in: water, fruit, sandwiches, Mars Bars, Lucozade, puncture outfits, inner-tubes. I go through everything and, satisfied it's all there, pull on my baseball cap and leather riding gloves. I test-ride my bike up and down the road. I'm ready! Nigel and Keith have both decided to wear cycling helmets, which is probably a sensible thing to do. I had thought about borrowing my seven-year-old son's Dennis the Menace helmet, but it was miles too small, and I couldn't get it on my big head.

We check that we're all set and bid Daniel farewell. After a quick photo at the noticeboard at the start of the walk we're ready – or are we? All four of us nip into the bushes for a quick piss.

'Right,' says Keith, 'it's now 8.50 a.m., let's go,' and off we all pedal.

It's obvious even at this early stage how the pecking order is going to pan out. Keith and Nigel tear off, with Gary and I already the back markers. I've only cycled 50 yards when my chain comes off. I go through the gears, pedalling but going nowhere.

We all stop.

'Just my fucking luck.'

The others laugh. It only takes seconds to fix, and off we go.

From here, it's uphill with bushes either side. Already my rucksack is rubbing my shoulders. A long-coated German Shepherd dog appears from some trees on the right and bounds towards me, barking. 'Why me?' I think. 'Just my luck to have me arse ripped out me shorts by a dog, and I've only just started.'

It is quickly followed by two more dogs. I slow down and stop, frozen to the spot. The dogs head my way, growling and barking. They smell fear. A woman appears and calls the dogs off. All three run towards her and stand obediently by her side. Their huge teeth and pink tongues are covered in white foam as they pant heavily. They've had their fun for the day, frightening the life out of me.

'Do you know, you shouldn't be cycling on the Downs,' she says in a posh Lady Penelope voice.

'I hope cycling's allowed m'lady, only I'm going to Winchester,' I say.

She is not impressed by my Parker impersonation.

One of her dogs is raising its arse in the air and straining out a large turd.

'So you've banned cycling, but it's all right to let your dog shit everywhere, is it?' I shout as I pedal faster to catch up with the others, who, by now, are fast disappearing up a hill.

It's a long hard start and for a good ten minutes we cycle uphill, but there are great views of the sea and the town of Eastbourne out to the right. I go through my gears, but nothing makes this uphill ride in damp grass any easier. I can feel the greasy fried breakfast I had earlier moving around in my stomach. I feel sick. It could be the food, or maybe it's the worry that I won't last the day in the saddle. This is a shock to the system – no one warned me it was this tough. I'm gasping for breath and beads of sweat are running down my forehead. The fucking rucksack's still cutting into my shoulders, annoying me already. It's time to get off the bike and walk. We've covered less than a mile and I'm fucked. Breathing heavily, I push the bike until we reach the top of the hill. There are good views in all directions; East Dean and Friston Forest to the south, the whole of Eastbourne and along the coast out to Hastings to my right.

The sun is out now and it's getting very warm. I get back on the bike and head downhill towards the A259 road. Once across the road, the route goes past the Eastbourne Downs Golf Course clubhouse, and the Way passes through the middle of the course. The track is broad and chalky here, with gorse bushes dotted around both sides of the path, and it's level for a mile and a half. If you want to get to the Beachy Head Youth Hostel, take the track off to the right and head downhill in the direction of Eastbourne Old Town.

The Way leaves the golf course behind and rises towards Eldon Bottom. I'm into the swing of things now and my lungs are getting used to nearly bursting. The views are magnificent as we pass by Willingdon Hill, checking the map as we stop for a minute. We've passed a few local landmarks, like dew ponds, woods and benches with memorials written on them. We've been bombing along at a fair old pace, so things are flying past. After Willingdon Hill, there are very few gates, so the run down from Bourne Hill is particularly good, that is until we head downhill into the village of Jevington, which takes its name from the Saxon leader Jeva, together with the noun for tribe, '*ing*', and settlement or village, '*ton*'. In April banks of bluebells can be found in and around the village, the symbol that spring is upon us and summer is just around the corner.

My back wheel is buckled by a large lump of chalk which flies up off the ground as we ride along a narrow path. My rear wheel is now so out of shape that every time it spins it rubs on the back brake blocks, and this makes cycling even harder.

At the bottom of the hill there are a few cottages and a tarmac road. Turn right here and after 50 yards take a left up Church Lane. The Eight Bells pub is at the rear of the Norman church. The pub is very popular with locals and walkers alike, and everyone is sure of a warm welcome. Jevington is the village where the dessert Banoffee Pie is said to have been invented by the chef at the local restaurant, The Monk's Rest, in the early 1970s. We carry on up a narrow bridleway, leaving the church behind, then reach a multiple bridleway junction where the path levels out. We pass through some woods in the direction of Holt Brow. Haywards Bottom is out on the right and above that is Hill Barn, the remains of an isolated manure barn. Friston Forest, with over 2,000 acres of woodland, lies to the south.

We stop for a quick drink from our water bottles at the edge of Windover Hill. Below is the valley of Tenantry Ground and Deep Dean. There is a nice, cool breeze blowing and we get our first views of the Long Man of Wilmington, the largest representation of a human figure in Western Europe. This 240ft figure, cut into the chalk and grass slopes, can be best viewed from near the car park at Wilmington, where you can see a 180-degree sweep of sea which stretches from Hastings to Bexhill and across to Selsey Bill in West Sussex. Here, too, are the ruins of a Benedictine priory, and facilities include a picnic site and public toilets. Under a yew tree in the grounds of the parish church of St Peter and St Mary, a Saxon chieftain lies buried. It is said the 1,400-year-old tree has great powers, and it is a symbol of immortal life. We curve around the top of the Windover Hill and, aside from the annoyance of my back wheel, we ain't doing too bad. I'm beginning to enjoy myself now.

We've been cycling for about two hours. Keith and Nigel are always out in front, trying to race one another. Well, they have got all the gear on, the tight Lycra cycling shorts and the matching multi-coloured T-shirts, as worn in the Tour de France. Keith even has a proper water dispenser, complete with plastic tube straight to his mouth – what a poser! Gary is about half a mile behind them, with me a couple of hundred yards behind him. What happened to our idea that we must all stick together?

We are now going downhill towards Alfriston, travelling along a narrow chalk path. My front suspension takes the main shock of the battering caused by the uneven track we're on. Bits of rock and stone fly into the air, flicked up by the speeding wheels of the others in front. Dust gets into my eyes and I slow down. I don't fancy ending up tangled in the barbed-wire fence that's running alongside me. We cross the road near a bridge and cycle alongside a stream, which runs parallel to the Cuckmere River. It's very muddy along here, making it impossible to cycle, and so we walk until we come to Plonk Barn where there's a small bridge over the stream, where we stop and take a few photos. I take one of the other three standing on the bridge. I can't get them to smile, they all look so fed up and knackered. 'Cheer up, you shirt-lifters, and smile,' I say.

I put my camera away and join them on the bridge. Down below in a field are two men lying naked in one another's arms. One of them jumps up when he hears us.

We leave the lovers and cross the white metal bridge which spans the Cuckmere River, then go through the small town with its narrow main street and small bric-a-brac and tea shops and pick up the South Downs Way at the side of the Star Pub. A small sign high up on the wall opposite the pub points you in the right direction.

From here it's up the King's Ride towards Bostal Hill. There's a chalk trail here, with rutted, deep pot-holes. The locals call it 'Bastard Hill' and after 100 yards of trying to get up it I agree and decide to walk. A man passes me as I push my bike. 'Keep going, son,' he says, 'you've only got another hour before it levels out.'

'Thanks, mate, I need cheering up,' I say.

'Don't you know anybody with a helicopter?' he laughs.

In front of me are Nigel and Keith, arses in the air, pedalling away. Gary, who's just yards in front of me, also gets off and walks. He waits for me and we walk together. We both agree it's harder than we thought. The sweat pours from our brows as we take a sip from our water bottles, which are already nearly empty.

The sun is out and I'm down to my last drop of water. At least walking I can take in the sights. I look back towards Alfriston and above the Downs where we've just come from, at the green hills sweeping down into the village. Gary decides he wants to start cycling again. Me, I'm happy to walk. I've got my Timberland hiking boots on, the boys have already given me stick for wearing them – they reckon I look like the builder in The Village People, but I knew they would come in handy.

At the bridleway junction, just before Bostal Hill, the others are waiting and we break out the first Mars Bars of the day as we stop and rest for five minutes. Just below Bostal Hill is Jerry's Pond and New Pond, both dried-up dew ponds. The ancient burial grounds around these parts have long since been dug up and robbed, and the Victorians and their notorious digs, which were big business in those days, have left a scar on the landscape.

Next we pass the car park at Bopeep Bostal. We pass through a couple of wooden gates, holding the gate open for each other. Now we're in a field full of sheep. Keith shouts to them that he's not Welsh and there is no need to worry. The sheep scatter as we thunder by. It's a gentle climb up to Firle Beacon, and there are good views of Lewes from here out towards Offham chalk pit. Charleston Farm and Firle Tower can also be seen. The ground is level and dry as we make our way through the car park above Blackcap Farm. There are more sheep everywhere as we pick up speed heading towards the radio masts at Beddington Hill, which, with the barren landscape and the wire fencing around the compound that houses the masts, has a touch of *The X-Files* about it. Again, I'm at the back.

It's downhill from here, and we slow only to pass through one or two bridle gates. Newhaven Port and the sea are out to the right and we pass the White Lion and Red Lion ponds. My back wheel is getting worse and I have to adjust my back brakes to stop the buckled wheel from slowing me down. The others don't wait for me. If I lose them, I'm fucked; we've only one map between us, and Nigel has it. I quickly jump back on the bike and follow them as they disappear over the brow of Itford Hill. Straight in front, down below in the valley, is the village of Southease. It's a quick descent, and as the Way curves around we head downwards until we are running parallel with the River Ouse. We slow down to pass a walker on the narrow chalk path. The stroppy bastard sees us coming but still won't move out of the way. We manage to squeeze past

Mr Helpful and dismount to go through a series of metal gates.

Down below we can now make out Southease church and railway station, and just off to the right is the village of Rodmell, which, at the bridge that crosses over the River Ouse, is an alternative route for walkers.

I finally meet up with the others at the bottom of the hill, where the busy A26 road crosses the route. After crossing carefully, the path carries on through the farmyard about 100 yards along on the left. There is a water tap here and a horse trough. We all fill up our empty bottles and have a swig of cool, fresh water, then carry on down towards Southease railway station, where we cross the railway line via the concrete bridge that connects the platforms. It is possible to use the two gates that allow cars to cross over the tracks, but it's easier and safer to do what we have and go up and over.

As we leave the station behind and go over the metal bridge that spans the River Ouse, we peer through the railway sleepers laid out for the base of the bridge, and see below us the green-coloured, fast-flowing river. We pass a farmyard on the left and stop outside Southease church, with its medieval stone wall. The picturesque church stands on the village green. A man sits at an easel, painting a pastel-coloured thatched cottage opposite the church, and as we set off again we pass him.

Nigel points at the cottage and shouts back to Keith, 'That's nice!'

Keith shouts back to Gary, 'Nice place,' and Gary shouts back to me, 'Fucking lovely, isn't it?' I nod in agreement. The man looks up, takes off his white panama hat and wipes his brow with a handkerchief, which he pulls from the top pocket of his cotton jacket – we've disturbed his peace. We come out onto a main road at the top of the village and turn right, and then left 50 yards along. There's a sign here for the Telescombe Youth Hostel. The path goes through a wooden gate, through a field with grazing horses and out through another wooden gate onto a tarmac road which leads to Beaky Bottom Farm. Before we reach the farm we go through a wooden gate, off to the right and up a steep hill. Cow shit and mud a foot deep make it impossible to ride so we push the bikes up the hill. When we reach the top we scatter the cows that are blocking our exit out onto the road near Mill Hill House, and exchange a greeting with two Harry Potter lookalikes who are packing away their tent and camping equipment.

The route leads down a narrow path between Hill House and some properties opposite. The path here is dry and after 200 yards we come out into open countryside. There are good views off to the right of Lewes. We continue north-west through a succession of bridle gates. Out to the left there is a view of Beaky Bottom Farm from a different angle. At Whiteway we cross the Greenwich Meridian Line and pass from the eastern hemisphere to the western. The Way now becomes a concrete path, which rises as far as the eye can see. There are acres and acres of yellow flowers.

I'm sweating my nuts off as I struggle to keep up with the others. Keith and Nigel are just dots in the distance. I stop to take in a drink. 'What the fuck am I doing here?' I ask myself. But I don't answer. Instead I wipe my brow with the back of my hand, take off my baseball cap and pour water over my head. 'Fucking hell,' I say out aloud as I get my sore arse back onto the saddle and pedal. I notice that Gary, 200 yards in front of me, has also stopped and I begin to catch up with him. He sees me coming, climbs back onto his bike and pedals away 19 to the dozen as he tries to manoeuvre his bike back up this seemingly never-ending hill.

After it seems we've been ascending for hours, the ground eventually flattens off. As I turn left a hay barn comes up ahead, and I find Gary there having a drink and hiding from the burning sun in the shade. I have another gulp of water and suck out the drips from the bottom. I had only just filled it up at the farm's water tap, but because of the heat my supplies are dwindling fast

'Where have the other two got to?' I ask.

'You know them,' says Gary. 'They're probably racing one another, they could be anywhere between here and Winchester, so let's get going.'

We both lift our already tired limbs onto our bikes. It's downhill here and a nice breeze blows in my face. The sea is a couple of miles out in front and we're heading towards it.

Something tells me we are going the wrong way, but I say nothing and we carry on. Maybe we *are* going the right way, but where are the other two? There's no sign of them. We carry on past the gravestone of a man who dropped dead while out walking on the Downs over 100 years ago. We pass a group of people catching butterflies in nets and stop and ask if they've seen two men on bikes come along this way.

'Was one of Asian appearance and wearing a turban?' asks one of them.

'I don't think so,' I laugh and they get back to catching their butterflies.

'We're lost, Gary,' I say and he nods in agreement. He pulls his mobile phone from his rucksack and rings Keith.

'I don't fucking believe it,' he says. His phone doesn't seem to have a signal. We look out over the surrounding countryside, scanning the hills and valleys for any movement.

'I don't believe it,' Gary repeats. 'How the fuck did we lose them?'

'Well, I was following you,' I tell him, excluding myself from any blame.

The path we're on is very overgrown and it looks like no one has passed this way for donkey's years. We decide to turn back to where the barn was, where we had turned left at the end of the long concrete path.

Gary's phone rings. It's Keith asking where we are. He tells Gary that they turned right at the end of the concrete track. We tell them where we are and they say they'll come down to meet us.

I lead the way back up towards the barn where we stopped for a drink, chatting away to Gary about getting lost. Then I realise that I'm talking, but he's not answering. I look back and he's not behind me. I turn the bike around and cycle back towards the gravestone we passed on the way down, only to find Gary lying flat out with his bike beneath him. Trying not to laugh, I ask if he is all right. He doesn't look up or move, but answers, 'I got the front wheel caught in a fucking rut, which must have been cut into the ground by a poxy farm vehicle, and I went straight over the handlebars and landed on top of the bike.' I'm now pissing myself with laughter as he gets to his feet and brushes himself down.

'I've had enough,' he says, 'this ain't for me.'

I wipe the tears from my cheeks as Keith and Nigel arrive.

'I just fell off,' mumbles Gary, red-faced. We hold an enquiry as to how we got split up. Keith says he was following Nigel, Gary says he was following Keith, and I say I was following Gary. It seems no one is to blame so we head back uphill past the barn where we had gone in different directions. We've added one and a half hours to our journey. Lesson one is to stick together, as Bryan Ferry sang.

We eventually get back onto the South Downs Way at Swanborough Hill. Here we stop for a bite to eat and I grab a drink off one of the others. We sit and look at the patchwork green fields of East Sussex. The views are something else. I close my eyes and relax. I could quite easily fall asleep. My head is resting on my rucksack and my mind and limbs feel as though they are drifting away as the sun warms my face and body.

'Right, let's go,' says Keith, jumping to his feet. By the time I'm up and standing, and on my bike, Keith's off and has put 300 yards between him and the rest of us. We follow, trying to catch up. Is this a race?

We pass the Kingston Hill Dew Pond. A little further on we fly at high speed past two more ponds. It's downhill and there is really no time to take in the scenery. We send sheep scattering as we pass along Juggs Road, an ancient trail which was the main route between the coast and Lewes market. Below and to the right is Cold Coombes. Hundreds of sheep graze peacefully on the sides of the steep valley. A wooden gate halts our fast descent, but once on the other side, it's business as usual as we speed downhill. Again a wooden gate brings us to a halt and once through the woods, the Way levels right out. We go through a brick tunnel that passes under a railway line, and the A27 road is 100 yards in front of us. We notice a petrol station on the far side of the busy four lanes of traffic, so off goes Gary to get some drinks and something to eat.

We've been cycling now for almost five hours and we all study the map closely, looking to see which way the trail takes us. A middle-aged lady approaches us on horseback, a small Jack Russell-type dog running alongside her. The first thing we notice is the size of her bust – she has huge tits and an ample portion of cleavage on display.

'Afternoon, chaps,' she says in a rather Hooray Henry accent.

'Hello, love,' I reply.

She stops the horse and asks if she can be of any assistance. I can't take my eyes off her thrupenny bits. We explain to her that we are cycling to Winchester on the South Downs Way, and that we had noticed on the map that the old South Downs route on the other side of the A27 was downgraded to a public footpath in May 1997. The new path takes you past Housedean Farm, near to where she lives, the lady tells us. She bends down further and one of the buttons on her blouse pops open, and her white lacy bra struggles to hold her heaving bosom in place. She doesn't flinch and seems far from embarrassed.

'Where are you staying tonight?' she asks.

'Anywhere you like,' I say, 'so long as it's with you.' Now she blushes, smiles and digs her heels into the horse's side, then moves off.

'Good luck,' she shouts as she, the horse and the dog disappear under the bridge below the railway line.

'I'd rather ride her than the horse any day,' I say, and the others laugh.

When refreshed with the drinks Gary brings back from the garage, Nigel and Keith think it's best to take the old route. I ask why, when the lady on the horse has just explained that the old route has not been used for well over three years and is overgrown and almost impassable.

For some reason, though, the other two decide to ignore her advice. With some difficulty we manage to cross the A27 with the bikes, near the petrol station. We run across the four lanes of traffic and stand on the central reservation as cars zoom past at high speed, only inches away. If we had taken the new route, we would have crossed the A27 via a footbridge that spans the road. We go through a gate and head up a steep hill. Cycling is almost impossible so we push our bikes up the grassy bank. At the top, Ascombe Farm is out to the right, behind us is the A27 and in the distance we can see Swanborough Hill and the radio masts at Beddingham Hill.

We carry on through some woods and emerge into a field of cows. The trouble is they are blocking our path and are standing around the gate we need to get through to carry on. We gingerly walk towards them, pushing our bikes. One of them moves and then they all move. I wonder if one charged, would they all charge? Safely through the gate, we're now in a field of five-foot-high wheat – just what I need with my hay fever. We follow the small path cut through the crops, and immediately my eyes start watering, the back of my throat gets dry and my nose itches. I sneeze and then sneeze again.

'Whose fucking bright idea was it to come this fucking way?' I shout, but no one can hear me as the other three are pedalling furiously uphill and are pulling away from me. We come to a gate where we all stop for a drink.

Here the new route for the South Downs Way comes in on our left. I take off my rucksack and dig out my hay fever tablets. I take one with a mouthful of water.

'Just what I need,' I say sarcastically, 'a field full of wheat to make me feel better. The woman on horseback was right; the way we've just come hasn't been used for years.'

Keith and Nigel don't say a word. Silence is golden. They both know we should have gone the other way. There's just enough time to wipe the sweat from my brow before we're off again, and this time, just for a change, we're going uphill. This is Balmer Down and it's uphill until we reach Blackcap, where the trail sweeps sharply around to the left. It's nice and flat along this stretch with good views out towards Plumpton Race Course and the agricultural college.

Just before Streathill Farm at Plumpton Bostal, a tarmac road leads down to the Half-Moon pub. Opposite the pub there is a shop and a post office. We decide to give both a miss and head through more grazing sheep and cows. It's been a lovely hot summer's day and we've seen no other cyclists, and only a handful of walkers. The views down below are magnificent. Little villages and farms are dotted on the landscape. This is what cycling on the Downs is all about. There's the odd steep hill along this part, but it's a comfortable ride. We pass along the western brow and the car park at Ditchling Beacon comes into view. Before the car park there's a dew pond on the left – as you go through the gate be careful crossing the busy country road that leads down into the outskirts of Brighton.

In the car park is the welcome sight of an ice-cream van. Keith puts down his bike, goes across and buys four cornets, each with a flake stuck in the top. They don't last long as we lick away trying to quench our thirsts. We sit down and have a breather; after half-an-hour's rest we're on our way again. The ice-cream vendor certainly does a good trade. The car park is full of people sitting in their cars eating ice-cream or sucking on frozen lollies while taking in the views. No doubt 2,000 years ago there would have been a vendor selling apples and jugs of mead to weary travellers, pilgrims and shepherds, and Roman soldiers. How things go in circles – the ice-cream man tells us he is from Rome. We pass the information board in the corner of the car park and head through the nature reserve run by the West Sussex Wildlife Trust. Out in front of us are fine views of the hills around the Devil's Dyke and the trees at Chanctonbury Ring. The views down below are stunning. Beyond the downland villages you can see out to Burgess Hill, Haywards Heath and as far as the North Downs. Now I'm enjoying myself. The pace has slowed, a breeze has got up, and I'm taking in things around me.

We reach Keymer Post. This is the point where you pass into West Sussex. The sails of the Jack and Jill windmills at Clayton are ahead, about a mile away. It's downhill so we get some speed up. Don't ask me how, but at this point we manage to come off the South Downs Way and miss the windmills, and end up on the A273. We follow this to the left then take a right past some riding stables and end up at the top of Woltonsbury Hill. Nigel reaches for the map, so it's odds on we're lost. He frowns and a worried look appears on his face.

'By the looks of it, we should have followed the Way around to the left, towards New Barn Farm, just before we reached the windmills,' he says, not looking up from the map.

'What fucking windmills? I never went past no windmills,' I say. Nigel is still mumbling away to himself. He's even got the map upside down. Perhaps he's thinking of a South Downs Way in Australia. Still, the bottom line is we're well and truly lost. We crowd around the map. Down below us, about a mile away, is the M23 London to Brighton motorway and on our left is a disused chalk pit. The only other way down is a trail leading to two farms, so we head downhill and turn left parallel to the motorway.

After half a mile we stop. Keith and Nigel both say that they think we're going the wrong way, so we turn round and go back the way we've just come. What a fucking balls-up! We stop and ask a farmer for directions. He's not sure, so we head out onto a bridge which goes over the M23. Once on the other side we're on a tarmac road. The signposts send us either towards Henfield, Small Dole or Horsham. Henfield and Small Dole, according to Gary, are the other side of Bramber and Steyning and from there we should be able to pick up the South Downs Way. We can see the hills of the South Downs, where we should be, off to our left about three or four miles away, but getting back onto them is another matter. The sun is going down and it's getting cooler.

We cycle along country lanes for a couple of hours until we reach Bramber. I can almost feel my arse smile with relief as we stop and get off the bikes. A mutual decision is made to find somewhere to stay for the night. We try the first pub we come to, but they are full up – no room at the inn. We go through the village and try the Castle pub and hotel, where Keith stayed the last time he cycled the Way. He pops inside and comes back out smiling. Bingo! We're in luck – they have rooms, so we book in. Keith and Nigel have decided that they are sharing a room, so me and Gary are in together. I suppose it's some sort of pecking order. The kings of speed, the champions of the hills, in one room, the slow bastards, the bike-pushers, tossers and hill walkers in another. I throw my bag on the floor and lie down on the bed, then pull off my boots and socks. It feels good to get some air around the old tootsies. Gary switches on the telly. The football is on, France v Italy. I watch, but I'm barely able to keep my eyes open. I ache all over and feel absolutely sold out. I'm fucked.

We've done 50 miles today, although looking at the map we've missed out a large chunk of the South Downs Way proper, including the Clayton Windmills, the Devils Dyke and the Steyning Bowl. My arse is red raw from riding all day but after dragging myself into the shower I feel a lot better. I stand under the hot, relaxing water for ages, then wrap a towel around me and slump back onto the bed. I could quite easily drop off to sleep, but there's a knock on the door from Keith so I get dressed and we all go down to the bar and have a few drinks and a bite to eat. We did contemplate having an Indian – there's one next door to the pub – but the last thing you need up on the Downs is a touch of Delhi Belly, so we give the Ruby Murray a miss.

The locals in the bar look at us as though we've just arrived from another planet. There's the usual country mixture of landowners with ruddy cheeks and beer bellies clutching pints of real ale, their wives standing alongside them with their highlighted blonde hairdos, matching pearls and cashmere cardigans, sipping on gin and tonics and showing just a bit too much cleavage, four-wheel drives parked outside in a position where everyone can see them. A tall man in a blue pin-striped suit with over-sized blue tinted spectacles, wearing a red dickey bow and red braces, talks loudly about the City's money markets. He's telling a man with a thin weasel-looking face to invest in the futures market, blah, blah, blah. The man seems to be having trouble staying awake, stifling a yawn with the back of his hand. A group of men in green wax jackets sit huddled round a table. One has a small roll-up fag dangling from his bottom lip.

The barmaid, with a Farrah Fawcett hairstyle which went out of fashion about 25 years ago, can't quite get the hang of my south London accent. When I order a drink it takes a while for her to register what I've said. She asks me where I'm from as she passes me the drinks I've ordered and hands me my change. 'I'm from Moscow, I'm Russian,' I tell her, and she believes me and says she wondered where my accent was from. The others turn away and laugh.

The pub food is excellent. We all have steak and chips, and sit outside enjoying the meal and a few drinks. After a few pints Nigel decides to turn in for the night, funny decision that, as it's his round. We tell him that not only can he not read a map, but he's a tight-arse as well. Keith buys a packet of condoms from the machine in the toilets and shows Nigel and the rest of the pub. 'I'll be up in a minute Nige,' says Keith, laughing. Nigel shakes his head and heads off upstairs to bed. Keith is in hysterics, but me and Gary can't see for the life of us what's so funny. We have a couple more drinks and then turn in for the night.

On the way to our rooms we ask the landlady if it would be possible to have a couple of rounds of sandwiches to take with us in the morning. 'No problem,' she says. My legs just about manage to get me up the stairs to my room and as soon as my head hits the pillow, I'm gone.

CYCLE SHOPS

Nevada Bikes, 1 Green Street, Eastbourne
  Tel: 01323 411549
Heath Cycles, 106 Cavendish Place, Eastbourne
  Tel: 01323 733404
Phoenix Cycles, 219 Seaside, Eastbourne
  Tel: 01323 729060
Les Smith Cycles, 192 Terminus Road, Eastbourne
  Tel: 01323 639056
Cycleman, 46 Rosebery Avenue, Hampden Park, Eastbourne
  Tel: 01323 501157
Re-Built Cycles, 7 Compton Street, Eastbourne
  Tel: 01323 417117

Sports and Cycles, 26 Clinton Place, Seaford
   Tel: 01323 893130
Halfords, Unit C, The Drove, Newhaven
   Tel: 01273 515885
Sports and Cycles, 1 Meeching Road, Newhaven
   Tel: 01273 513647
Lewes Cycles, 28 Western Road, Lewes
   Tel: 01273 483399
The Bicycle Workshop, 28a Park Crescent Terrace, Brighton
   Tel: 01273 677390
Rayment Cycles, 13/14 Circus Parade, New England Road,
   Brighton Tel: 01273 697617
On Your Bike, 126 Queens Road, Brighton
   Tel: 01273 821369
Freedom Bikes, 96 St James Road, Brighton
   Tel: 01273 681698
Halfords, Unit 1 Pavilion Park, Lewes Road, Brighton
   Tel: 01273 604883
Ridgen Cycles, 3 Upper Gardner Street, Brighton
   Tel: 01273 681861
Planet Cycles, Madeira Drive, Brighton
   Tel: 01273 695755
Splash Mountain Bikes, 5 Middle Road, Shoreham-By-Sea
   Tel: 01273 440727
Les Smith, 72 Boundary Road, Portslade
   Tel: 01273 411180
Raleigh Cycle Centre, 38/42 Kingston Broadway, Shoreham-
   By-Sea Tel: 01273 596368
The Henfield Cyclist, 2 Bishops Croft, The High Street,
   Henfield Tel: 01903 495900
Norvett's Hike and Bike, The High Street, Alfriston
   Tel: 01323 870485

HOSPITALS
Eastbourne District General Hospital, Kings Drive, Eastbourne
The Royal Sussex County Hospital, Eastern Road, Brighton

YOUTH HOSTELS
Beachy Head Youth Hostel Tel: 01323 21081
Alfriston Youth Hostel Tel: 01323 870423
Telescombe Youth Hostel Tel: 01273 301357
Patcham Youth Hostel Tel: 01273 556196
Truleigh Hill Youth Hostel Tel: 01903 882204

TOURIST INFORMATION
(Phone for a full list of hotels and B&Bs)
Eastbourne Tel: 01323 411400
Seaford Tel: 01323 897426
Lewes Tel: 01273 483448
Brighton Tel: 01273 323755
Hove Tel: 01273 778087
Shoreham Tel: 01273 452086

The Cycle – Day Two
BRAMBER–SOUTH HARTING

THE SOUND OF RUNNING water stirs me from my sleep. I open my eyes slowly, and it takes a few seconds to work out where I am. Then my brain kicks in and reminds me that the previous day I did a 50-mile cycle ride. I turn over and the whole of my body aches. Gary's bed is empty; he must be in the shower. I look at my watch – it's 8 a.m. Fucking hell, he's a bit keen. I close my eyes and tell myself, 'Just another ten more minutes, ten more minutes and I'm sure I'll feel better. Then I'll get up.'

I drift off back to sleep, but I'm woken again by Gary's voice. Am I dreaming? I open my eyes and see Gary dressed and on his mobile. By the sounds of it he's talking to Sharon, his wife. I rub my eyes and stretch my limbs. Gary bids farewell to the lovely Sharon and throws his mobile on the bed. 'Morning Kingy,' he says, starting his hairdryer and looking in the mirror, combing his wet locks.

'Can't you sleep or something?' I ask him, turning over yet again.

'The early bird catches the worm,' he says.

'What fucking worm would that be?' I ask. 'The only worm you've ever seen is the one you had in your hand before you fell asleep last night.'

I get up in slow stages, first pulling my legs up to my chest and then sitting on the edge of the bed. Step three, I stand up and stretch my hands, trying to touch the ceiling.

'The shower's nice and hot,' says Gary, putting the finishing touches to his well-coiffured hairstyle. I manage to get my brain in gear and have a shower.

Afterwards I get dressed and pull on my boots and lace them up. It's only day two but already I hate the sight of them – they only remind me of the pain I suffered the previous day. Then it's downstairs for breakfast. Every slow step is painful. The other three are already tucking into a hearty fry-up. The food is again very good and we decide to hit the road. We pick up our sandwiches, wrapped neatly in tin foil, from reception and pay the bill, £25 for the bed and breakfast and a fiver each for a couple of rounds of sandwiches per person – that's what I call good value for money. The rooms are comfortable, clean and tidy and the food is excellent.

We pick up our bikes from the garage where they were locked away for the night, but I ain't looking forward to getting back on the saddle. My chad are still sore from yesterday and the cheeks of my arse feel like they're on fire. If I meet an Irishman today and he says 'How's the crack?' I shall drop my strides and show him – my arse is like a baboon's. I ride around the pub car park and if anything my back wheel has got worse. It's hard work even pedalling on the flat. There is no way I am going to get up and down some of the hills up on the way. As we tinker about with my wheel, a man delivering to the pub tells us that there is a bike shop in nearby Steyning. Both Keith and Gary think they know where the bike shop is, so off we cycle in search of it. The rucksack on my back immediately gives my shoulders gip; yesterday the pain in my legs made me forget the irritating problem with my backpack.

We leave Bramber, a beautiful little village, behind and

head into Steyning, which is literally a 10-minute cycle away. Steyning is also a lovely place – both villages are well worth a visit. We find the cycle shop in the high street. It doubles as a car accessory shop. I push my bike in, with the others trooping along behind me, and tell the man behind the counter the problem.

'Leave it with me,' he says, 'and I'll sort it.'

'Also the gears ain't too clever, can you have a look at them?' I ask him.

'No problem, me old mate,' says the man. 'Come back in half an hour and I'll have it done.'

'You good at fiddling then?' asks Keith.

'Yes, I am,' he replies, 'I don't pay VAT.' He remains straight-faced as he answers.

We walk out of the shop laughing.

Gary says he knows a good baker's just a couple of hundred yards along the high street so we pop in there for some supplies. We've already got some sandwiches from the pub, so we just grab some drinks and cakes. We have a stroll around the village looking in the shop windows as the locals go about their daily business and then head back to the bike shop.

'All done,' says the man as soon as we enter the shop. 'I've put on a new back wheel and I've tried to get the gears changing the best I can. But to be honest, they are far from perfect.'

'How much do I owe you then, mate?' I ask, pulling some scrunched-up notes from my back pocket in anticipation of a huge bill.

'Give us a score,' he says as he wipes his oily hands on a piece of cloth.

'£20, are you sure?'

The man looks at me, puzzled.

'That's well cheap,' I tell him.

'I can charge you more if you like,' he replies, straight-faced for a moment before a huge grin spreads across his chops.

Keith asks if he can buy some oil for his chain.

'Help yourself to a can off the shelf,' he says.

I hand the man a £20 note and take out some more change to pay for Keith's oil, but he cheerfully insists that it's on the house.

We all thank him and shake his hand, telling him what a gent he is and how he has saved our trip.

'Good luck with your journey, boys, it was a pleasure to have helped you.'

'What a nice man,' says Keith as we close the front door of the shop behind us. 'It just goes to show there are still some good people left in the world.'

We all agree it makes a change to meet someone so helpful.

We leave Steyning behind and after looking at the map head towards Washington, where we plan to join the South Downs Way somewhere just before Chanctonbury Ring. As we head out of town, I realise that for the first time I'm out in front – perhaps my new-found confidence is due to the fact that my bike's working properly now, and I might just be able to keep up with the others.

A lorry loaded with scaffolding passes us and sounds its horn. The driver drops his window and shouts out 'KINGY!' I wave to him, not even knowing who he is because I didn't get a proper look at him. Further up the road the wagon comes to a halt and out of the driver's side steps my mate Westy, a fellow Chelsea supporter who drinks in my local pub. He laughs to see me miles from anywhere, riding a bike.

'I never had you down as a keep-fit fanatic, Kingy.'

I spin him a story that the others are having trouble keeping up, and I'm only taking it easy so that they don't feel as bad. The others stand there open-mouthed. They can't believe what they're hearing here. 'What a fucking cheek,' I can just hear them thinking. We chat for a while and then carry on our journey.

I drop back to my usual position of bringing up the rear as we follow the A283 past Wiston Park. Just before Lower Chanton Farm we take a left up towards the car park at Chanctonbury Ring. The tarmac road soon leads into a single dirt track, which rises through woodland. I'm off the bike and walking now as the ground gets steeper. The others are well in front of me and for once I don't care. My mobile rings and I stop to take the call and have a breather. This part of Sussex I know quite well, so I can't see myself getting lost. Once out of the woods and at the top of the hill the countryside opens up and I see the other three sitting on the ground, trying the sandwiches.

'What took ya so long, Kingy? Try one of them sandwiches the woman at the pub made. They're not cheese and pickle, they're more sweet pickle with a dash of cheese,' Keith says.

I take off my backpack and slump down beside them then, carefully unwrapping the sandwiches, I lift one out. Brown pickle oozes from the wrapping as I pull the silver foil back.

'Fucking hell, she's gone a bit mad with the pickle,' I say, laughing. I take the top layer of bread off. Inside is a small piece of cheese the size of a fifty-pence piece, drowned by what must have been nearly a jar of sweet pickle.

'They're all the same,' says Keith, looking over my shoulder at what I've uncovered.

As we sit munching away on the brown stuff a horde of schoolkids appear from over the brow of the hill and head towards Chanctonbury Ring. It's misty and the sky is grey, but it's hot and humid and walking up the first steep hill of the day, pushing my bike and talking on the phone at the same time, has me sweating. Off we go on the bikes and we soon catch up with the schoolkids, passing the distinctive clump of beech trees at Chanctonbury Ring. This place has a strange feel about it.

Just past the Ring, the Way rises to 780ft, passing a fenced-in dew pond before sweeping round to the right 200 yards on. We now begin to go downhill. Sheep graze in fields on either side. At the Scarp Foot lies the village of Washington. Be careful as you descend on this stretch of the Way, as it bends down a steep flinty track. We pass a gas sub-station and can hear the sound of the traffic from the A24. There's a car park at the bottom with an information board. The Way carries on directly opposite, on the other side of the A24. Great care should be taken when crossing this busy road. Instead you can turn right for an alternative route and follow the road into Washington, where walkers and riders who wish to avoid the dangerous A24 can turn west at the village, go past the church and cross the bridge over the A24. Continue to Rowdell House, where you turn south and then south-west up the hill to where you rejoin the South Downs Way at Barnsfarm Hill.

We like to live dangerously and cross the four lanes of traffic on the A24. We pick up the Way by going up Glazeby Lane and going around to the left past the water point opposite Bostal Hill Farm, and then climbing gently upwards onto a tarmac road. This turns into a flinty track which runs through a wooded area and then into open countryside. A building which looks like something from *Dr Who* comes up on your right. It is in fact an army building left over from World War Two. Worthing and the sea can be seen off to the right as we climb higher. The sun breaks through and we stop for a drink from our water bottles and catch our breath at

Barnsfarm Hill, where the alternative route rejoins the Way.

It's 12.30 p.m. and we've been cycling for an hour and a half since we left the bike shop at Steyning. We pass Sullington Hill, then a Dutch barn and cattle troughs before going through the car park at Chantry Post. There are a series of metal cattle grids along this stretch so you have to concentrate fully when cycling over them, or better still dismount. After leaving the car park behind, it's a steady climb up Kithurst Hill, where there are some good views of nearby Storrington. Now we're heading downhill towards another car park, which is at the bottom of Springhead Hill. Parham House and park can be seen clearly from here; it's the annual steam rally today, which attracts visitors from all over the country. From Springhead Hill to Rackham Hill the Way is almost level.

From the top of Rackham Hill you can see across to Bury Hill, and where the River Arun winds its way from Amberley to Pulborough. It's nearly all downhill from here, with only the odd gate or stile slowing you down. Downs Farm is on the left with hundreds of cattle in the surrounding fields. Even in the summer the Way is very muddy on this section, although a lot of the brown stuff ain't mud, it's cow shit, so tread or ride with care. Amberley chalk pits come into view, now an open-air industrial museum. Go through another bridle gate and down a bumpy stony path; the exposed roots of nearby trees make the surface very uneven. At the bottom take a right past a large mansion house called Highdown. Here the Way takes another turn to the left. A road runs off to your right with a sign for a shop, and you are now going down a little road called High Titten. At the bottom you meet the B2139 road.

As we descend down High Titten, a coachful of schoolkids pulls out in front of us. Keith decides to race it to the bottom. You can see the coach driver looking in his wing mirror as if to say, 'What's this mad man on a bike playing at?' Keith overtakes the coach and raises his arm in the air, victorious. We follow the coach down, keeping our distance from the clouds of black smoke belching from its exhaust. At the road junction the coach goes right towards Storrington and we go left towards Amberley station. We go past the museum under the railway bridge and meet Keith sitting outside the small tea-room next to the River Arun. We prop our bikes up against the flint wall, remove our cycle helmets, take a deep breath and plop down on the wooden seats to take in the sun.

'Well that made a change,' I say, 'us lot sticking together today.'

I get up and go off into the café, coming back five minutes later with a pot of tea on a tray, the cups and saucers jangling and chinking. It was nice and cheap as well, a bargain at only a fiver.

'Five fucking pounds?' says Gary. 'What, for four cups of tea? The place must be twinned with Harrods.'

We sit and relax for 45 minutes and after looking at the map and filling up our water bottles from an outside water tap, we're back on our journey. Amberley was the place we were aiming to reach at the end of day one, and if we hadn't got lost around Clayton Windmills I think we would have made it.

We cross over the River Arun via the stone bridge at Houghton and follow the road past a church and farm buildings on the left. We take a right turn between some cottages and a group of farm outbuildings and are now on the road to Bury village. The signs for the Way are 200 yards on, on the left. The path is chalk and very dusty and dry, and rises quite steeply with good views out to the left of Bury village and behind Amberley and Houghton. The trail down from Rackham Hill can be seen in the distance and the surrounding farms are dotted on the landscape.

The temperature is rising quickly and even Keith and Nigel have taken to pushing their bikes. We head uphill past Coombe Wood and stop and chat to a man walking towards us. He's walking from Bury Hill, where we are now, to Bramber, which is about 20 miles away. He tells us he's cycled the South Downs Way twice before and now walks it in stages. We wish one another well and carry on pushing our bikes the last 200 yards to where we meet the A29 road near the top of Bury Hill.

The Way goes right here and then, after 50 yards, turns left up a slight hill and then out into the open countryside. From here you can see the car park and refreshment bar at the very top of Bury Hill, which most weekends is full of hundreds of bikers of all ages showing off their machines and colourful leather outfits. They queue in a very orderly fashion for teas and coffees. It looks like the Village People are making a pop video here! According to the others, my boots fit in well.

We carry on downhill past open farmland with Eartham Woods and Houghton Forest off to the left. Farm vehicles have cut deep ruts into the trail and it is quite difficult to cycle along this stretch. I should know; I had trouble staying on my bike and came off here, going over the handlebars and landing headfirst in the mud. I picked myself up and wiped the dirt off my face and hands with my T-shirt, but luckily no one saw what happened, so I climbed back on my bike without having the piss taken out of me. I laughed to myself – if I'd seen any of the others do the same they would never have heard the last of it.

At the bottom of Westburton Hill there are some barns and outbuildings. A huge, brown, murky puddle slows our progress. Once through the cack-coloured waters it's a steep climb up towards Toby's Stone, as we climb the steep zigzag track. Only Nigel managed to cycle all the way to the top. The wonderfully named wood of Egg Bottom Coppice is below you. Toby's Stone is a memorial stone with an inscription for 'James Toby Wentworth Fitzwilliam, Secretary of The Local Hunt'. The views behind and out to the left are splendid; much of the land to the west is owned by the National Trust.

From Bignor Hill we make our way to the car park, where we sit propped up against the large wooden signpost. From the south, and running up and across the Way, is Stane Street. This Roman road was built in AD 70 to connect London with Chichester. Down below is the Roman Villa at Bignor and out to the south the spire of Chichester Cathedral can be seen. We tuck into the last of the pickle sandwiches. One mouthful is enough for me and I launch the rest over my head and into the nearest bush – let the sparrows have it. Before long my eyelids are drooping and I'm in the land of nod. Laughter from the others wakes me up. I open my eyes.

'You all right?' says Keith, smiling. 'You were snoring your head off there.' The car park begins to fill up with people giving their dogs a walk and we decide to crack on.

I drag my weary body onto the saddle once again. Nigel says he isn't feeling too well and thinks he's got a cold coming on, Keith complains of feeling light-headed and Gary's worried about how his hair looks. Me, I've only got the arse ache. Off we go. I try to change down to a lower gear but nothing happens. I click away on the gear change on my handlebars. Now I'm stuck in one gear – the cog on the back wheel for the gear change won't go up or down. What else can go wrong?

We pass the signs for Gumber Farm, a camping barn owned by the National Trust. The trail is now a broad farm track, level and dry. There are good views of the sea and you can see as far out as the Isle of Wight. More sheep in a field scatter as we ride through them. On the right are two radio masts, which can be seen as far back along the Downs as Bury Hill. We head along Scotcher's Bottom and down towards Littleton Farm and the A285. At the road junction turn right and then directly opposite pick up the South Downs Way. The sound of barking dogs fills the air. The lane rises towards a bridle gate. I get off and walk. I look behind and the barking dogs have come out through a gap in a hedge and are chasing towards us up the lane. Keith's holding the bridle gate open and me, Nigel and Gary are through it like a shot. The gate slams shut and we're all on our bikes and pedalling like the clappers. Trouble is, we're cycling across a ploughed field and uphill and I've only got one gear and don't seem to be moving. It's like treading water. I look across my shoulder and the dogs are less than 50 yards behind and closing. Sweat pours off my brow and I cycle like mad. They're now less than 20 yards away and getting closer. 'Fuck this,' I say, and I stop. I bend down and pick up a piece of stone. To my surprise the dogs stop, and stand and bark. I lob the stone at them, firing a warning shot across their bows, and to my surprise they turn around and run, only to stop after 50 yards, turn round and head back towards me, barking. I bend down again and pretend to pick up a stone, and they turn and run. 'Fucking cowards,' I shout. The dogs have had their fun and head back towards where they came from.

We pass through another bridle gate and head uphill towards Stickings Pit Bottom, then out through some woods and past a large wooden signpost. Out to the right there are good views of Seaford College down at Duncton. Now we're travelling along Graffam Down, where the path is broad and dry. We've been going along at a steady old pace. The sun is out but a nice breeze is blowing and despite the fact that I'm still stuck in one gear, I'm enjoying the ride.

This section of the Way is very wooded and the views out onto the weald on the right are spectacular. There's a distinct lack of sheep and cows along this stretch. We see a couple of wooden towers which look like something from a German prisoner-of-war camp. In fact they are platforms constructed by the Cowdray Estate for deer shooting. Cocking Down comes into view as we leave Charlton Forest behind. Now we pick up speed once again as we bomb downhill towards Hill Barn Farm. Halfway down the track turns to chalk with deep ruts and large loose stones. It's becoming pretty dangerous to stay on the bike, but this doesn't deter Keith, who cycles like a mad man. We pass the outbuildings of the farm, past some cottages with their windows and fascia boards painted in a disgusting, sickly chicken-korma colour.

We come to a halt at the junction with the A286. Keith is already lying on a grass bank at the side of the road as the three of us stop together. We put down the bikes and stretch out on the grass. Nigel complains of feeling unwell and Gary's concerned about finishing the whole of the cycle by tonight – he doesn't really want to spend an extra night away from home.

The time is now 4.30 p.m. At the most we have about five hours of daylight left. We've covered about 30 miles today and, to finish it, we need to set off now to cover the last 30 to 40 miles to Winchester. A decision has to be made. Nigel wants to quit now and cycle his way home to his house in Bognor Regis, which is only about 17 miles away. After studying the map, me, Gary and Keith suggest carrying on to Harting Down, about two miles from civilisation, where Keith's son Daniel could pick us up and take us home. We can carry on tomorrow from where we finish tonight. Phone calls are made to inform our wives that we will be home tonight. 'Don't rush back,' we are told. 'Us girls are having a barbecue.'

Keith phones Daniel and arranges for him to pick us up in a pub near Harting Down. We cross the road and pick up the South Downs Way next to the car park opposite. We pass Crypt Farm with more yellow window frames and head up a steep chalk lane with high hedgerows either side. I'm not even going to attempt to ride up here. Me and Gary talk as we walk side by side pushing our bikes. I can walk faster than my gears will allow me to ride. Keith and Nigel, never ones to be beaten, are standing up in their saddles and forcing themselves and their bikes up the hill. At the top, to the south, you can see the grandstand at Goodwood racecourse, along with the two radio masts on the hill next door. The path now levels out, with woodland to the south and good views of Cocking village to the north. The trail cuts through fields with wire fencing both sides of the Way. We go through a bridle gate and into some woods above Monkton House. The Way sweeps left as you come out of the trees. The grassy mounds of the Devil's Jumps are on the right. After 200 yards the path goes around to the right. It's a broad track along here through Philliswood Down. As you descend towards Buriton Farm there is a disused pit to the right. Before the farm, the Way takes a sharp right and you head towards Mount Sinai and Pen Hill. We nearly missed the turning for the Way near Buriton Farm as me and Keith were chatting, and it was only Gary waiting at the signpost that stopped us missing the turning. Pity Keith and Nigel didn't think to do that yesterday, when we got lost for an hour and a half.

At the bottom of Pen Hill we stop for a breather. We need to psych ourselves up for yet another steep hill. It's nearly 5.30. Nigel is feeling ill with a cold. He's gone a funny colour and Keith feels light-headed and looks white, so he eats a couple of Mars Bars and drinks a bottle of Lucozade I have in my bag to get some sugar into his body. He's so bad that he has the shakes. I clear the last of the apples from my rucksack and give them to Nigel. He devours them in seconds, core and all.

Again we walk up the grass slopes of yet another hill. Looking back down onto Buriton Farm and the surrounding areas, you can imagine how lonely life would be if you lived up here. At the top of Pen Hill you can see the villages of Elstead and East Harting. Beacon Hill is in front of us. At the bottom of Beacon Hill the Way curves down to cross a dyke. We follow the contours of Beacon Hill towards Telegraph House, which is steeped in history. We're now on the other side of the bottom of Beacon Hill. The trail has taken us along a less steep route than going directly up and over Beacon Hill.

We continue to Bramshott Bottom, where there is a large wooden signpost set in concrete at the head of the valley. We're not too sure how to follow the signs; the ones for the Way are a little bit misleading. Gary's getting the hump and just wants to get home. He isn't bothered about which path we take, but the trouble is we could end up miles from where we want to be if we choose the wrong one. We decide to head uphill through some scrubland and emerge onto the vast open spaces of Harting Down. We picked right – we're lucky for a change.

The green copper spire of South Harting church can be seen in the village at the foot of the Downs. Out to the west there is the radio mast on top of Butser Hill. The woodland of the Queen Elizabeth Park lies below it. There is a wooden bridle gate and we're in the car park of Harting Down.

Day two's over. We've covered nearly 40 miles and are

about 30 miles from Winchester. If only we hadn't got lost up at Swanborough Hill. If only I hadn't got a buckled wheel. If only my gears hadn't packed up. It's all 'if onlys'.

Daniel picks us up at the arranged pub just along the road from the car park, and tells us the landlord wasn't sure about serving him because he has his work clothes on. We have a couple of pints just to quench our thirsts and then drop Nigel off at home before going for a carvery meal in a pub near Aldwick, which is just outside Bognor Regis. As I walk in, my mate Westy, the scaffolder, is propping up the bar. He can't believe he's seen me twice in one day, and tells the pals he's with how he saw me earlier in the day in a little village.

Keith and Gary shake their heads. 'Please,' pleads Keith, 'no more bullshit'.

From there we meet the girls at the barbecue and finish off the night with a few more drinks. We all agree we will have to finish the ride another day, tomorrow's out of the question as my bike needs fixing, Keith and Nigel ain't 100 per cent and Gary's got a hair appointment.

Next day I'm having trouble getting out of bed. The whole of my body aches and I can just about move my legs. I ache in places I never knew I had. We've got a day's ride still to do to complete the cycle of the Way. But when will we complete it – if we ever do?

CYCLE SHOPS

Les Smith, 31 Chapel Road, Worthing
    Tel: 01903 201956
John Sponner Cycles, 21 South Farm Road
    Tel: 01903 232884
The Storrington Cyclist, The Forge, 38 West Street, Storrington
    Tel: 01903 745534

The Steyning Motor and Bike Spares, 116 High Street, Steyning
   Tel: 01903 812919
City Cycles, 44 Bognor Road, Chichester
   Tel: 01243 539992
Les Smith, 38 The Hornet, Chichester
   Tel: 01243 771713

HOSPITALS
Worthing General Hospital, Lyndhurst Road.
St Richards Hospital, Spitalfield Lane, Chichester

TOURIST INFORMATION
Worthing Tel: 01903 210022
Fontwell Tel: 01243 543269
Bognor Regis Tel: 01243 823140
Chichester Tel: 01243 775888

LOCAL ACCOMMODATION
Bramber Castle Hotel, Old Tollgate Hotel, The Street,
   Bramber
Tottington Manor Hotel, The Street, Bramber
Springwell Hotel, High Street, Steyning
Chequer Inn, B&B

The Cycle – Day Three
HARTING DOWN–WINCHESTER

ALTHOUGH A FEW WEEKS had passed since we finished the cycle at Harting Down, I was determined to complete the cycle of the South Downs Way. I had my bike serviced and a new gear changer and various other parts replaced, but I still wasn't 100 per cent happy with it. To me, it still didn't feel right. I'd also got over my aches and pains, from which I had taken a good couple of weeks to fully recover. Me, Gary, Keith and Nigel all came up with various dates on which to finish the ride, but one thing or another would crop up and the ride would be cancelled and put back for another day. As that date approached, yet again a new date would be made and that in turn would be cancelled. If two of us could make it, the other two were busy. This went on and on and on, until I took the bull by the horns, or the bike by the handlebars, and said 'Fuck it, next Friday I'm doing the ride.' The other three couldn't make it. It looked like I was on my own, but that didn't bother me as I was determined to finish the whole route and I liked my own company. It also meant I could do it at my own pace; with no one to race against, I could just plod along. It was going to be perfect.

But then Keith's 14-year-old son Tom said he would like to come along. I didn't mind that, Tom's a good kid who likes a laugh and has a good sense of humour, and he's just like his old man – he'd want to finish the ride from Harting Down to Winchester no matter what.

At seven in the morning, Keith and Tom pick me up and we load the bikes into the back of his van. After a good fried breakfast at a roadside snack van just outside Chichester, we head off for the South Downs, which is less than ten minutes away. We arrive at 8 a.m. at the deserted car park at Harting Down. The sun is shining and the grass is covered in the fresh morning dew. We look down towards South Harting, where me and the boys finally finished after a tough two-day cycle from Eastbourne. I for one couldn't do as much as I wanted to that day because my bike was stuck in one gear, and Nigel had been suffering with a heavy cold and was laid up for a few days after. Gary and Keith had sore arses and the bollock-ache, so there were four good reasons why we packed it in then. But today I'm going to finish it, that's for sure.

By 9 a.m. Tom and me are ready to go. We shake hands with Keith, who as usual says he wishes he were coming with us.

'Well, go home and get your bike then,' I say, pulling my hand from his grip.

'Go on, fuck off!' he laughs and off Tom and I go. We ride out of the car park across about 50 yards of grass and pick up the Way, then head towards the B2141, which is the road we've just come on from Chichester. We've only been on the bikes for 30 seconds when we have to dismount and cross the road, and then we're going downhill again, following the signs for the South Downs Way.

The chalk, flint single track here is wet and slippery so we have to take extra care, though soon we pick up speed and pass Tower Hill off to our left. The tarmac road we have just crossed is now 200ft below us on the right. After a couple of minutes we're off the bikes again to cross the B2146, which goes down to Uppark. Again the South Downs Way faces us. Carrying on through a small car park we follow the track, which along here is quite muddy. This track is called Forty Acre Lane. In parts, where it is dry, it's possible to get some speed up. We follow the green signs with the acorn on for about a mile. At a tarmac road, which runs across the Way, we go straight ahead past the stables and Downland Farm and then uphill towards Hundred Acre. Out to the left is the forestry plantation of West Harting Down. We cross the Sussex border path just north of Foxcombe Farm. From here there are some good views back to Torberry Hill and out towards Petersfield.

It's downhill now, but beware – before you reach the tarmac road, which goes into Sunwood Farm, the track is very muddy, forcing us to dismount. We turn right at the farm and head uphill. At the top there is a sign for Ditcham Park School, off to the left. We take the right fork, which goes downhill around a sharp bend, and on the left is Coulters Dean Nature Reserve. There is a sign here telling us that the reserve is home to rare butterflies, orchids, milkwort and squinny wort. I've have met and been out with a skinny sort, but never a squinny wort!

We carry on past Coulters Dean Farm, going under the power lines and up a steep gravel hill, and can now see the fast-moving traffic on the A3 Portsmouth to London road out in the distance. We go downhill past some cottages on the left. A caravan is parked at the front of Dean Barn. At the end of the track there is a road and facing us is Halls Hill, belonging to the Forestry Commission. The Way carries on through the wooden gate at the end of the small car park and up a very steep hill overlooking Faggs Farm. The road we have just crossed is New Barn Road, which will take you down to Buriton, less than half a mile away, or you can carry on to Petersfield, about two miles away. Tom and I get off our bikes and push them up the steep hill, which is a mixture of chalk and mud, very wet and slippery. There is no way you could cycle up here. Not even Tom's dad or Nigel would have any joy. At the top we stop for a breather, take our bags off and have a drink. There are good views back towards South Harting and beyond.

The road is flat and dry for about half a mile and then the track leads into the Queen Elizabeth Country Park. Here the South Downs Way splits into two, one path for walkers and the other for horse riders and cyclists. At this point there are numerous routes going in every direction and it is quite confusing, but the South Downs Way is well signposted and we bomb downhill through the woods for about a mile. Birdsong can be heard above the droning sound of the traffic on the A3, which runs through the far side of the park.

As we reach the car park at Gravel Hill Bottom, Tom slows down and realises he has a puncture. We stop and Tom takes his wheel off to try repairing the puncture, but it's no good, nothing will inflate the tyre. He has come well prepared with spanners and other tools which he pulls from his backpack. I'm most impressed, at least until he tells me the spare tube he has with him is the wrong size. We try for over an hour to make a repair, but the repair kit cannot cover the size of the hole in the inner tube. Tom seems to think it may have happened earlier when he skidded coming downhill through the woods.

I phone Keith on my mobile and explain what's happened. Our luck's in, as Keith is working in Portsmouth, which is only 20 minutes away. He is going to find a bike shop and run a new inner tube down to us. I've bought two inner tubes with me, but they won't fit Tom's new all-singing, all-dancing sex machine. We wait outside the information centre for Keith, who turns up within the hour and replaces the tube.

We are off once more on our travels, though we've been held up by the puncture for over two hours. As we leave Keith behind in the car park we go past a sign that says 'Winchester 21 miles'. Our route takes us under the A3, via a tunnel, and at the other end carries on past a public toilet near a bridle gate. Then it's into open fields, very steep in the direction of Butser Hill, where we are heading. Halfway up there's a gate. Pass through this and take the left-hand path. The car park, café and water point are off to the left in the direction of the mast, which can be seen for miles around. This area is well used by hang gliders, grass skiers and model aircraft flyers, and after dark by courting couples.

Tom manages to get to the gate, cycling all the way up the steep grass hill. He is just like his dad, who also loves a challenge. I'm not so determined, and cycle halfway and walk the rest. There are good views back to the information centre and along the A3 down towards Portsmouth. The leaves on the trees in the park are a mixture of golden brown, yellow, red, maroon and shades of dark and light green.

Passing through another bridle gate and a section of bramble bushes we come out onto Limekiln Lane and are now onto a tarmac road. The Way runs parallel to the road. There are good views over Oxenborne Down and Hampton Hill. At the crossroads the tarmac road goes to the left, so we take the right-hand fork along a gravel track that heads in the direction of Tegdown Hill. After a while the Way becomes a shingle track.

My mobile rings, and as I stop to answer it the heavens open and the black skies tip down on us. I end my call quickly and stuff the phone back in my jacket pocket. Within seconds of the rain starting I'm soaked right through. We head towards the two radio masts at Wether Down, but before reaching them we go through some woods which come out at Hyden Cross, where on clearer days there are some good views to the right of East Meon church. Here the road goes in different directions, to Clanford, Horndean, Druxford and East Meon. We shelter under the trees for a few minutes to take a look at the map. It's pissing down with rain, and the roads have rivers of flowing water cascading down the ditches which struggle to carry away the volume of water. It's not going to ease off by the looks of it, so it's back on the bikes and off we go again. How can such a sunny morning have turned into such a wet day? At nine this morning it was perfect weather, now you wouldn't catch a duck cycling in these conditions.

The Way goes straight on and you pass by HMS Mercury, which is a naval base. It seems a bit strange to have a naval base about 20 miles from the sea and up one of the highest hills on the South Downs. At the far end of the wire fence, which runs around the base, the Way runs right down a muddy track. There is a mast in a field on the left and a little further along, near Wetherdown Barn, there is another. It's downhill here. We pass a man and woman walking their dog. They had passed us in Queen Elizabeth Country Park when Tom had his puncture, and they nod and say hello.

You have to be careful along this stretch as it is very wet and muddy, and deep ruts have been cut into the trail by farm vehicles, Tom has already come off once and got soaked by a puddle, just before he got his puncture, and did I laugh? Of course I did, and he wasn't too happy.

We gingerly head off down Salt Hill and over Coombe Cross, then turn left at the signpost at Henwood Down. Be careful not to go straight on here as you will end up in the middle of nowhere, which is easily done. From Henwood

Down, head downhill towards Hall Cottages. The track here becomes a concrete path with good views straight ahead of Old Winchester Hill. Take a right at the bottom along the road that leads to Whitewool Farm. Go past the barn and metal feed hoppers on your right, then take a left along the road which skirts the farm. Cross over a brick-dammed pond and carry on for about 300 yards, then turn right through a series of metal farm gates.

We decided to stop here and shelter under a tree from the heavy rain, but it was hardly worth it as we were soaked to the skin anyway. I only had on a sweatshirt with a T-shirt underneath and my tracksuit bottoms and boxers were wringing wet. I really should have brought some waterproofs. Tom has on just a thin lightweight top, which is hanging off him with the weight of the water it has soaked up and splashes of mud have been flicked up his back by his back wheel. We wait here for five minutes and have a Mars Bar each. I shake off some of the water and ask Tom what he thought of the Queen Elizabeth Country Park.

He looks at me rather blankly, with a puzzled expression on his dirty, wet face.

'What park?' he asks, wiping the remains of the hair gel off his hands as he flattens his normally spiky hair down. 'I never saw no park.'

'The Queen Elizabeth Country Park, where you got the puncture,' I say.

Tom laughs. 'I was looking for a kids' park with a slide and swings!'

He means it too.

We climb back on the bikes laughing hysterically and immediately below the disused chalk pit we turn right and up a muddy single track. To our right we can see the masts at HMS Mercury, and back to where we have just come from.

It's a one-mile, steep, slow climb until you reach a wooden gate. Go through the gate and you are out onto a tarmac road. Here the Way splits, with cyclists and horse riders having to take an alternative route up Old Winchester Hill Lane. Despite lengthy negotiations and a public enquiry, there is still no agreement on a permanent route for the South Downs Way between Old Winchester Hill, Beacon Hill and the Meon Valley, so until such time as there is, horse riders and bikes should follow the distinctive green signboards on the roadway.

We head off to the right and the route is downhill for a couple of miles. The rain is pissing down and we are both drenched to the skin. We only had a short stop at the chalk pit at White Wool Farm and if we hadn't got the puncture earlier, I think we might well have finished by now and have missed some of this rain. We could probably have done today's ride in about four hours.

At the bottom of the road the route gets very confusing. We are now on the A32 and opposite is the George and Falcon pub. After studying our map we decide to turn left. After 100 yards there is a road on the right, and a blue sign with a white acorn. The map did say they would be green, but any colour will do. The sign says 'Winchester 10 miles', so we head in that direction.

After about a mile there is a lawn mower repair centre on the left, then a forge and a sign for the South Downs Way. Behind the forge, go up a hill to find two gates at the top. One indicates a bridleway to the right, and the road straight ahead is a private one. Take the bridleway and turn immediately left. Follow the trail across a field until you come to another gate, then carry on into some woods in a clearing. Here you will find a small car park with a tarmac road running in front of you. Walkers may now rejoin the Way through a metal farm gate on the left. The various routes for the South Downs Way merge into one here.

Take a right along the road. After 200 yards the Way goes off to the left and becomes a stone track. Lomer Pond is hidden behind trees on the right and there are some cottages on the left. The trail is downhill until you reach Lomer Farm. Again, the Way is not very well signposted here, and with various different lanes and paths running off behind farm buildings it is easy to miss the exit. We have to ask the farmer, who is very nice and points us in the right direction.

We're back on course and it's downhill towards Wind Farm, with more barking dogs as we go through the farm, past the woodpile and turn left out onto a tarmac road. The South Downs Way runs parallel to the road, which we decide to stay on due to the heavy rain. We pass by the entrance to Preshaw House, where Love Lane runs down through some large gates to the Preshaw estate. Half a mile up the road there is a crossroads and taking a turn left here will take you down Salt Lane, but we turn right. There is a sign for Shaun Coper Antiques. Millbury's restaurant and pub comes up on your right. As far as I know this is one of the few pubs which are actually on the South Downs Way, though there are loads near it. The pub, once called the Fox and Hounds, has a treadmill which used to draw water from a deep chalk well inside. It is a good place to stop for a rest and draw breath. Tom and me press on. Anyway, he's too young to drink.

Just past the pub the Way turns left past a couple of houses, and we pass a new one called Green Gable. We follow the tarmac road down to a barn where the South Downs Way goes straight on at a gravel track; the tarmac road sweeps right down in the direction of Hamilton Farm. It's muddy along here in places, as the use of farm vehicles has made the trail uneven. I come off my bike twice within a minute and I'm covered in mud. Tom finds this very amusing and is in fits of giggles, the big tart, though to be fair I did laugh at him when he came off. The rain eases off as we cross Balls Lane track and drop into Holden Farm, then go past the farmhouse and the various outbuildings.

At the top of the farm track is the A272 road, which we cross. The trail carries on uphill for about 200 yards and then goes through a farm gate. Follow the signs, which are clearly marked, to take you around the edge of the field. At the top of the open field is another gate. Ganderdown Farm is out on your left. Pass through a double field gate. There is a barn on the left and we head down towards Keeper's Cottage and farm. At the farm I give Tom the chance to read the signs, which point in different directions. We go straight on, Tom's choice, and somehow we manage to get lost. We soon realise something ain't right so out come the maps and we discover we are sitting outside Turnpike Cottages, down near the A31. According to the map we are travelling in the wrong direction so we head back uphill towards Keeper's Cottage and, after studying the map yet again, turn right. This means that we should have turned left at the farm coming up from Rodfield Lane, where the hay barn was. It's uphill now through the woods. As we leave the farm and cottages behind we are on a double farm track, which is quite dry. It's a straight ride with Temple Valley on the left. We come to a wooden gate and head through the woods at Great Clump. Here the Way becomes a single mud track and only with great difficulty do we manage to stay on our bikes. There is barbed wire fencing on either side, so extra care must be taken to stay upright. At the end we come to the A272 road, which we've already crossed once, outside Holden Farm. Cheesefoot Head car park is on the left.

Pick up the Way directly on the other side of the road in

front of you. There are good views of Winchester and, off to the left, of Southampton and beyond. The rain stops and the sun comes out. The Way turns right and runs downhill, and Telegraph Hill can be seen to the right. It's up and down, and dry and then muddy, along this stretch. We're heading towards Deacon Hill. At Little Golders you come to a flagpole and a warning sign for army ranges. Somehow (my fault) we make a mistake. We should have turned right here and taken the tarmac road that runs down into the village, but instead we take the path that runs alongside the danger area at Deacon Hill. We follow this path, with trees on either side, for about two miles. We should have gone through the village of Chilcomb, but instead we come out onto Morestead Road. We can see the city of Winchester below us and we cycle off downhill. At the bottom we go under the M3 flyover, around a roundabout and down Bar End Road heading towards the city centre and the end of the South Downs Way.

My mobile rings. It's Keith, waiting for us at the end of the South Downs Way. By the directions he's giving me it sounds like we are only minutes apart, I check my map and try to find where Keith is waiting for us, and get back onto my bike only to discover I've got a puncture. Shit! I pedal on regardless. I get about 100 yards when Keith and Tom's brother Daniel pull up behind us. Keithy boy leaps from the van and pops the cork on a bottle of champagne he's brought with him. 'Well done, King,' he says, shaking my hand. 'You've done it.'

And I have – I've cycled the South Downs Way from Eastbourne to Winchester. It has taken me three days in total, including today's six-hour soaking, taking into account punctures (only one between five of us in three days) and bad map-reading. We hadn't done too bad overall. During the three-day ride we have had some bad luck, or should I say *I've* had some bad luck, with buckled wheels, gears not working and getting lost. I think I have done rather well to finish it in just three days. How the fuck did Keith's doctor friend and Peter with the dreadlocks at the yacht club finish it in just one day? Well, now Keith and I have both done the whole route. That just leaves Nigel and Gary, but it seems they are still thinking about it. Dream on, boys.

I strip down to my boxer shorts and climb into the passenger seat, next to Keith, who's driving. He puts the heaters on full blast and the hot air begins to dry me out. Tom passes me a dry sweatshirt from the back and I slip that on. It's not long before I'm drifting off to sleep. The next thing I hear is Keith talking into his mobile phone, telling whoever it is to run a hot bath because 'your man's' only 15 minutes away.

'Oh, don't be like that,' I hear him say.

'Who you talking to?' I ask him as I open one eye. Keith just smiles and laughs that unmistakable Keith laugh.

CYCLE SHOPS

Halfords, 149/150 High Street, Winchester
   Tel: 01962 853549
Peter Hansford, 91 Olivers Battery Road, (South) Winchester
   Tel: 01962 877555
Hargroves Cycles, 26 Jewry Street, Winchester
   Tel: 01962 860005
Les Smith, Unit 4, Andover Road, Retail Park, Winchester
   Tel: 01962 856311
Owens Cycles, 22 Lavant Street, Winchester
   Tel: 01730 260446
Cycle World, 224a London Road, Waterlooville
   Tel: 02392 240087

HOSPITALS
Queen Alexandra Hospital, Southwick Hill Road, Portsmouth
Royal Hampshire Hospital, Romsey Road, Winchester

TOURIST INFORMATION
Petersfield Tel: 01730 68829
Winchester Tel: 01962 840500

PART THREE

The Walk – Day One

WINCHESTER–QUEEN ELIZABETH COUNTRY PARK

A LOUD BUZZING NOISE stirs me from my deep sleep. It takes a few seconds before I realise the sound is coming from the flashing alarm clock on the cabinet next to my bed. I fumble in the dark and hit the snooze button, then lie my head back down on the warm pillow and look at the clock. The bright numbers glowing in the dark tell me the time is 5.30 a.m. 'What silly bastard's set the clock for this unearthly time?' I think as my eyes begin to slowly close again, my brain telling me I need more sleep. I begin to drift back off into the land of nod.

Then another part of my brain kicks in and reminds me that it was me who set the alarm for this unearthly time and that today I was to start my walk along the South Downs Way. Keith is picking me up at 6 a.m. and following me as I drive to the Queen Elizabeth Country Park on the A3 near Petersfield, where I will park my car. Keith will then take me on to Winchester and drop me off at the start of the South Downs Way, so that when I've finished today's walk my car will be waiting for me at the other end.

I manage to struggle out of my nice warm pit and I'm ready and waiting for Keith when he turns up punctually. We make our way over to the country park, where I leave my car and climb into Keith's van. As we head off in the direction of Winchester, I double-check my rucksack to make sure I've packed everything: mobile phone, maps, sandwiches (cheese and pickle), Mars Bars (two), bottle of Lucozade, litre of still mineral water, two pears, two plums, tape recorder with tape, baseball cap and (after getting soaked on the last leg of the cycle last week) a white plastic half-length poncho complete with hood, which a drinks company gave away at Wimbledon a few years ago and has been at the bottom of my wardrobe until now. I knew it would come in handy one day, although I look a complete prat in it.

We park up in the centre of Winchester and after being pointed in the direction of a decent café near the bus station by a postman out on his round, we head there and order a full house special each, washed down with a couple of mugs of tea. I need to fill up with a bit of grub to keep my energy levels high on such a long walk, although I don't know what Keith's excuse is; he's a plumber and only needs his strength to count the loads of money he rakes in. The food is good and the place quickly fills up. We notice they have loads of photos of the Southampton football team and its players all over the walls. Matthew Le Tissier seems to be a particular favourite, as his face looks down from nearly every wall. I bet you don't get many Pompey fans in here.

After breakfast we drive over to the start of the walk, along the Petersfield Road. At the end of the road there are a set of bollards where the road ends and a footpath begins. About 50 yards along, a footpath runs off to the right. It looks as though somebody has tried to paint a blue acorn on the ground. The road goes on past some red brick houses on your left, with a children's playground at the end of the row. Turning left, there is a footbridge that runs over the M3 motorway but there are no signs telling us that this is the start/end of the South Downs Way. On the other side of the footbridge are open fields. I turn left, and in between a high hedge and the motorway down below I see the first sign telling me that I'm on the South Downs Way. This is where I leave Keith and he tells me he wishes he were walking with me, shakes my hand and wishes me good luck. I'm off. In front of me is a 24-mile walk. I'm nervous but I want to prove to myself that I can do it, and I'm excited because after the 100mph cycle ride the walk will allow me to take more in and enjoy the Downs at my own pace.

I leave the sound of thundering traffic on the motorway down below and head off into the open fields, following a muddy track. This section is for walkers only – cyclists and horse riders have to go via a track near Magdalen Hill Down and rejoin the Way in Chilcomb village. I check my watch. It's ten to nine on a bright, dry Tuesday morning in September. To my left, about half a mile away, is the A31 road and above that Magdalen Hill Down. The village of Chilcomb is a mile in front of me. To the right of the village I can see the Saxton church of St Andrew's, which still uses a bell that was cast in 1380, and the woods of Deacon Hill. A treatment works and some farm outbuildings and cottages are off to the right. The sound of the motorway has now disappeared and the stillness of the English countryside kicks in.

To my left there is a 100-yard stretch of fir trees that blocks out the A31. At the end of the field there is a stile. Go over that and turn right onto a tarmac road that runs into the village of Chilcomb. Pass the manor farm and follow the blue sign for the South Downs Way. Past Fawley Down Farm, carry straight on past the public phone box. The Way now rises quite steeply as you head towards the top of the hill at Little Golders. Carry on for about a mile

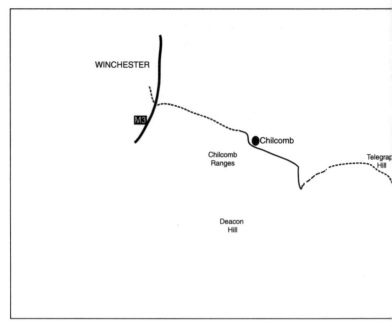

and as you reach the top, the South Downs Way sweeps around to the left and out onto a shingle track. Three green metal posts can be seen in front of you and to the right are a flag-pole and a sign warning of army firing ranges. This is where I made a balls-up on the cycle with Tom and went in the wrong direction.

Carry on up the farm track for about another mile, heading towards Telegraph Hill, where the views stretch across the Downs towards the coast and Southampton. There are hedges on both sides, but some spectacular views of Winchester out to the left and open farmland and woods to the right, which can be glimpsed through the gaps in the hedgerows. I can see a yellow flame leaping into the air from a chimney that sends plumes of smoke out into the now clear blue sky. A group of around 20 or 30 magpies fly into the air

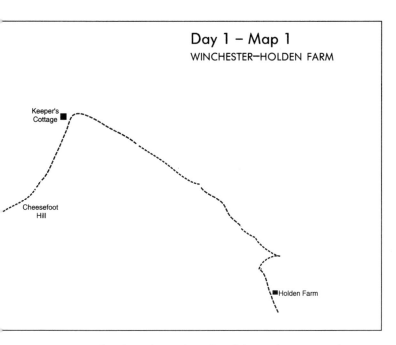

Day 1 – Map 1
WINCHESTER–HOLDEN FARM

Keeper's Cottage

Cheesefoot Hill

Holden Farm

as I pass by disturbing their breakfast. The A272, the A31, the M3 and panoramic views of Winchester can be seen from here.

I head down through open countryside past a long line of conifer trees, which smell fresh but damp. The path narrows to a single track and to the right a wood appears, curving around a valley. The only sound is that of birds singing and the breeze rustling the leaves on the trees. Chilcomb Down is off to the left and the car park at Cheesefoot Head comes into view. People out walking their dogs disappear into the nearby woods. The Way now cuts across a cornfield and in front of you the A272 cuts across your route. Southampton and beyond can still be seen to the right, but ahead and to the left are some amazing landscapes which stretch for miles and seem to reach as far as the North Downs, Box Hill and

Dorking. The view really is breathtaking. The sun casts shadows right across the valley to my left.

I carry on through a green metal gate and cross the A272. The Downs and open countryside are on the left, and a wooden signpost bears the name of Mike Heneghan, a sort of memorial. Out to the right, 50 yards away, is the car park and below that the woods of Great Clump, and 20 or so blackbirds fly into the air as a shotgun pops. The Way is a single track here, with bramble bushes and barbed wire either side. The path is extremely muddy. The landscape to the left dips down into a large valley, where sheep graze. The woods of Long Clump edge the valley and the path passes through woods down to a gate. On the other side the trail widens to a farm track. Temple Valley is to the left, where hundreds of pheasants cover the open land of cut corn fields, sharing their feeding ground with hares and rabbits. The pheasants are everywhere, thousands of them; they seem to rush out of your way at the last minute and disappear through gaps in the hedges. If chickens peck at insects in the grass, then pheasants must smoke it – they're daft birds. They not only act divvy, but they don't taste all that bright either, definitely an acquired taste. I head downhill and the last of the pheasants disappear into the hedgerows as Keeper's Cottage and the farm appear up ahead.

The Way turns right here and the A31 appears again to the left. A double track leads up a hill and down again towards Gander Down. I cross Rodfield Lane, which leads to Oving Down Farm, and see my first person of the day, an elderly lady walking a beagle and a spaniel. She bids me good morning and stops for a chat. The dogs come around me wagging their tails. I bend down and give them both a stroke and a pat. 'They can probably smell my two dogs,' I tell the old dear, and it seems she would be happy just to stand around and talk all day. She tells me she walks this five-mile route every day and that's what keeps her fit and well.

'I'm 84 years old,' she says proudly.

Why do old people always tell you their age?

I carry on up a slight hill where I stop, take off my rucksack and have a drink of Lucozade. I've been walking for an hour and ten minutes and have covered about three or four miles. I slip my rucksack back over my shoulders, and see that what looks like a mother fallow deer and her two young charges have stopped about 200 yards away and are watching me from the middle of a ploughed field. As I take a few steps towards them they take off into the distance, bounding almost like kangaroos as they disappear over the horizon.

I carry on down towards Gander Down Farm. A coarse 30ft-high hedge is swarming with wasps diving in and out of the red berries, which are hanging in huge bundles from the hedge – this is real Worzel Gummidge country, typical old English countryside.

At a hay barn, which comes up on the right, the direction to take becomes quite confusing, with one sign indicating the direction I've just come from and another pointing straight ahead, the way I'm now walking, but another pointing to your right. I consult my map, which tells me that straight ahead is the correct route. If you wanted to stay the night somewhere on your way towards Winchester, then I suppose the barn would be a good place to stop, but I'd ask the farmer first and, of course, no smoking in bed.

A black rabbit nearly trips me up as he makes a dash from one side of the hedge across to the long grass opposite. I come to a gate with sheep grazing near it. Holden Farm can be seen from the top of the hill as I cut through the middle of them. Down below, and just on the other side of the A272, clouds of smoke rise from one of the outbuildings on the farm and the smell of burning plastic hangs in the air. I can taste it in my throat. I close the gate to the field behind me and go down a short gravel lane. The smoke blows across the main road and up the lane towards me. Two riders on horseback trot past, covering their faces with one hand, and mumble a 'good morning' through their gloved fingers. I wonder if I'm doing the right thing going towards the thick, grey, billowing smoke, but there are no flames and no one's shouting for help. There doesn't seem to be anybody around at all, not that I could see them anyway if there were. I ain't turning back now.

The whole of Holden Farm is covered in a grey blanket of smoke as I cross the main road and cover my mouth with the map I am carrying. I cannot see more than a foot in front of me and the smell of burning plastic is disgusting. I run through the blanket of choking fumes and when I'm out the other side, in the fresh clear air, I can see a bonfire burning and plastic guttering and rainwater down pipes blazing away. Some silly fucker's burning a mound of plastic! If this was in town, the culprit would be nicked by the local environmental health people. Only the other day I was watching farmers on TV during the fuel crisis. I almost felt sorry for them, but I'm beginning to change my mind now, after nearly being gassed by burning plastic.

I carry on, and once I'm at a safe distance of a couple of hundred yards, I take out my water bottle and wash the taste out of my throat. I splash some water into my eyes, which have begun to sting. I rest up for ten minutes until I feel better and then carry on.

Heading towards Hamilton Farm I pass by a barn that would be an ideal place to stop and catch 40 winks if you wanted a rest. Further on there are two llamas in a field. They

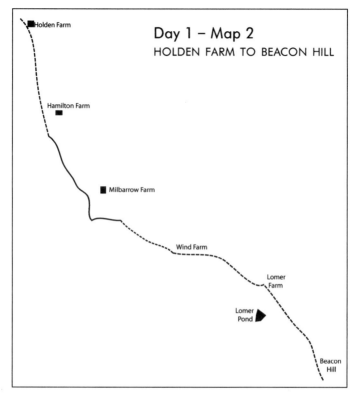

Day 1 – Map 2
HOLDEN FARM TO BEACON HILL

Holden Farm

Hamilton Farm

Milbarrow Farm

Wind Farm

Lomer Farm

Lomer Pond

Beacon Hill

stop and stare as I pass them. I say hello, but they don't move. Perhaps they don't speak any English, but my Spanish is only up to ordering large beers, or 'Where does the bus stop for the market?' They're both about 5ft tall, one beige and white and the other completely white. One reveals his protruding, yellow-stained teeth in a toothy Ken Dodd smile, and then the pair gallop off. Seeing these llamas reminds me that there's also meant to be a pair of wild ostriches along a part of the Downs. There's an ostrich farm on the Surrey/Sussex border, and apparently a couple of birds escaped and now the pair live happily roaming the Downs.

The Way is very muddy here and I pass the road that leads down to Hamilton Farm. Another hay barn is on the right. It's the fourth I've seen since leaving Winchester. I carry on up the tarmac road for about half a mile past a large bungalow on the right, called High Stoke, then turn right onto the main road after about one mile. I go past the Mulberry Inn and take the first road on the left. Coming along the field opposite me are two people leading donkeys with harnesses on. I carry on up the road for about one mile, then turn right into Wind Farm, go through the yard and pick up the Way. I stop for a drink and go down the lane, which is very muddy. I just manage to squeeze down the sides of the puddles without getting my feet wet. There's a cut cornfield to the right and Lomer Farm comes into view. Southampton and beyond can be seen in the distance. It's very peaceful and tranquil. If you ever need to get away from all the hustle and bustle, this is the place. Walking is so relaxing.

When you reach Lomer Farm, turn off slightly to the left and go past two cottages. The road goes off to the left. Take the right-hand fork with the pebbled track and head off up the slightly rising lane. There's a flint cottage on the right (Corner Cottage) and on the left, just behind some trees, is Lomer Pond. Carry on until the lane meets the tarmac road, and within 100 yards a car park comes up on the left. This is where the South Downs Way splits at Beacon Hill. Walkers, take the route directly in front of you through an iron farm gate and across a ploughed field. Cyclists and horse riders should take another route, which runs down towards Wheely Down Farm.

I carry on towards the Meon Valley and at the end of the ploughed field go over a wooden stile and turn left onto a single car-width tarmac road (White Way). Here the signs for the Way are almost non-existent.

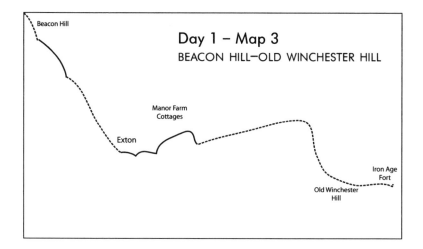

Beacon Hill

Manor Farm
Cottages

Exton

Iron Age
Fort

Old Winchester
Hill

I miss the sign, if there is one, which should have taken me back across the fields to my left, but end up carrying on along the road until I come into the village of Exton. It is all downhill and the views are splendid. To my left as I descend I can see right across the Meon Valley, and to the right is the view over the Punch Bowl, a miniature version of the Devil's Punch Bowl at Hindhead, near Guildford.

I arrive in Exton village. There is no sign of life. Although the place is deserted it is very picturesque, with lots of quaint flint cottages. I've seen no one for nearly an hour. I turn left into Church Lane and past the St Peter and St Paul church, which I stop to have a look at. If I were an artist this is the sort of church I'd sit down and paint in watercolour.

I turn to the right into Shoe Lane and pass the Shoe Inn pub, which has a public phone box opposite it. I then cross over a small bridge, below which are the flowing waters of the River Meon. I climb Beaconhill Lane. At the end of it the A32 road faces me and there's a bus stop opposite. A number

53 bus runs from here to Southampton, and on the other side of the road it is possible to catch a bus to Petersfield.

I follow the banks of the river and the A32 heading towards Manor Farm Cottages. About one mile along, across the main road, there is a sign indicating that this is the point to rejoin the South Downs Way. I cross the river, taking care because the path is slippy. Some old railway sleepers give me something to aim for as I hop from one solid foothold to another. Be careful not to get your feet wet; there's still a fair way to go. Shavards Farm, with its outbuildings and bales of hay, can be seen to the right in the distance.

Further along, the track runs through a dried-up chalk-bedded stream, but in winter the stream re-establishes itself very quickly. The Way passes under a disused railway line, through a red-brick arch. It's hard on the feet as the red-and-white granite chippings are difficult to get a good foothold on. My feet are starting to get sore. This section of the walk would be almost impossible to cycle on, and with the low hanging branches of the trees nearly touching your head, I should think horse riding would be a no-no.

After a mile of this type of terrain the Way now swings right and fields open out to both sides. I've been walking for five hours. As I look behind me I can see in the distance where I walked at the top of Beacon Hill two hours ago. It's uncanny, a strange feeling. It looks as though I've covered no distance at all.

My feet are blistered and aching. I contemplate stopping and pulling my boots off to give my feet a well-earned rest, but if my feet swell up I won't get them back on. I reach a wooden gate that leads to the nature reserve just below Old Winchester Hill and its Iron Age fort, which dates back to the second century BC and was used as a tribal meeting place for the region around the Meon Valley. The grazing sheep keep the grass on the reserve well maintained. You can follow the 'easy-going' nature trail around the hill, but dogs must be kept on a lead. The views from this point are superb; it's possible to see out towards the Isle of Wight and the New Forest and beyond. It's cloudy today, but with fine weather you'd see for miles.

The Way winds around the edge of the nature reserve and there is a wheelchair access point. There is a real sense of history up here. I shouldn't think the landscape has changed much for hundreds of years. As you head away from the Iron Age fort, the South Downs Way carries on along a gravel track. Follow this until you come to a tarmac road, Old Winchester Lane, then turn left out onto it and go straight ahead for about a mile. To the right, in the valley below, is White Wool Farm.

There is no footpath or bridleway to take a shortcut down to the farm from the road I'm on, so the trail follows the road then cuts through fields and comes out onto a farm track. The farm lies at the end of a lane, but first I pass through a series of metal gates. There are cows grazing on either side of the track and I turn left around the edge of the farm buildings at the end of the road then cross over Whitewall Pond, using the small brick bridge that leads to two big galvanised feed hoppers. Here I turn right and head towards Hall Cottages. Past these the Way turns left up a concrete road, which rises up towards Hen Wood. Down to the right in the distance is Coombe Cross Farm and its cottages. I can see the masts just outside HMS Mercury at Wetherdown on the hill in the distance.

I've been walking for six hours now and have covered about three-quarters of today's walk. My feet are soaking wet and I can feel the blisters coming up on both soles and the back of one of my heels. My legs feel heavy and the laces have

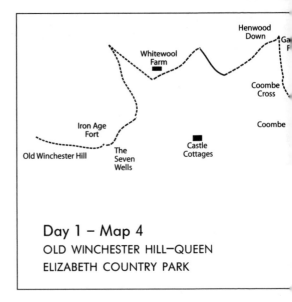

Day 1 – Map 4
OLD WINCHESTER HILL–QUEEN
ELIZABETH COUNTRY PARK

started to come loose on my boots, but I don't want to stop or I may have a problem getting started again.

At the top of Henwood my spirits are lifted when I get my first sight of the radio mast on the top of Butser Hill, which means there's not much further to go. Or is there? I can't tell.

There's a barn in front of me and the South Downs Way turns right here down a muddy path, which rises along Halnaker Lane. At the end of it I come to a crossroads, Coombe Cross. I pick up the Way across the tarmac road and go past the post box set in the wall, then duck under the metal barrier and follow the shingle track uphill for about a quarter of a mile. At the top of Salt Hill, the mast and barn of Whetherdown are on the left, and there are good views in all directions. On a clear day you can see the south coast and the sea.

The boundary fence of the HMS Mercury is on the left-hand side, and the Way turns left here and out onto a tarmac

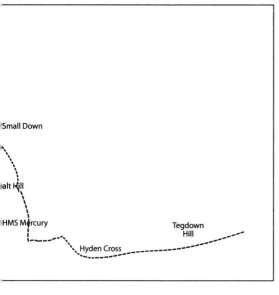

road which leads down to the main entrance of HMS
Mercury. Carry on past the base, and the road goes past some
newly built houses on the right. It's downhill here and at the
bottom there's a small island of grass. A signpost sends you in
various directions: East Meon, Druxford, Horndean. The
South Downs Way, though, is straight on. Following a
shingle track, you leave Hyden Cross behind and cut through
the edge of Hyden Wood. Local rumour has it there is a large
wild cat that roams these parts. It is said the black cat is either
a panther or a puma that escaped from a visiting circus and
has survived for many years by feeding on a diet of young
lambs, pheasants and chickens. Perhaps it holidays on
Dartmoor or Exmoor. Other people will tell you that the
beast is in fact a Rottweiler dog with an undocked tail, which
was either thrown out by its owners when it became too big
or lost while out walking. Anyway, I keep an open mind and
my eyes peeled.

It has now been seven hours since I left Winchester and apart from the odd few minutes' stop to take a drink or get some grub out of my holdall, I haven't really rested for any great length of time. I've used up all my water supplies and my thirst makes me want this walk to end. I've got the hump with it now. I've bitten off more than I can chew – 25 miles on the first day of walking seems now to have been a little too ambitious. Still, I must carry on. There's no mountain rescue up here on the Downs.

My throat's dry and even the muddy puddles seem to be inviting me to take a drink. I feel light-headed and my legs are like lead. I'm well and truly cream-crackered. Walking is now painful and I take small pigeon steps, because the insides of my legs are sore where they've rubbed together and the cheeks of my arse feel like they're on fire. I'm hurting big time. I just want to get to the end. I need water, and I need to rest. I gee myself up and tell myself I'm going to finish.

'Go on, keep going, don't give up. Don't be a loser,' I shout out loud.

I pass Tegdown Hill on my left. The track is wet and muddy, but on the ridge I can see the church at East Meon. The Way now comes onto a tarmac road. Take extra care here as the road is very busy with traffic heading towards the café and car park at the top of Butser Hill. I wish a car would stop and offer me a lift, but that's cheating. I must carry on. To take my mind off things I try to concentrate on the exceptional views of the Queen Elizabeth Country Park and the woods down below me. The busy A3 road can be seen in the distance.

Leaving the road I'm on, I hurry through a wooden gate and follow the trail to another gate. From here it's downhill to the car park where I'll finish, which is still about a mile away. Sheep graze peacefully and do not give me a second look as I pass by them. A group of rabbits feed undisturbed as I hobble within feet of them.

The open spaces of Butser Hill can be a lively place, and on some days you can see people hang gliding, grass skiing and model aircraft flying, but today there's just a solitary old lady walking her dog on a flexi-lead. I'm nearly on all fours as I tiptoe past her and my lips feel as though they're twice their normal size. I need water and quick.

At last I'm at the bottom of Butser Hill. Not far to go now as I pass the public toilets and go under the A3 and into the car park. My car is in sight, but I'm walking like a one-legged fucking pigeon, doing one small, calculated step at a time. I'm in agony. I pass the car and head for the information centre and café. My need for liquid refreshment is the only thing on my mind at this moment in time. What shall I have? Tea, coffee, an ice-cold Coke, a milkshake? I might even have a lolly or an ice cream. I take some money from my trouser pocket, slip the bag off my back and pull at the door – but it doesn't budge. I pull again. Nothing. I look at the sign, which says 'Closed 5.30 p.m.' I check my watch; it's 5.30 now, and I've been walking for eight and a half hours.

TOURIST INFORMATION
Winchester Tel: 01962 840500
Petersfield Tel: 01730 68829

TAXIS
A.P. Cars Tel: 01962 884713
Rivendell Tel: 01962 711811
Wessex Cars Tel: 01962 877749
Worthy Cars Tel: 01962 885990

PUBLIC TRANSPORT
Bus Station, Winchester (On the walk, the number 53 stops
   at Exton for Southampton and Petersfield.)
Railway Station, Winchester and Petersfield

YOUTH HOSTEL
Winchester Tel: 01962 853723

LOCAL PLACES OF INTEREST
The City Museum, The Square, Winchester
Winchester Cathedral, The Close
Marwell Zoological Park, Golden Common, Winchester
The Gurkha Museum, Peninsula Barracks, Romsey Road

The Walk – Day Two

QUEEN ELIZABETH COUNTRY PARK–COCKING

I SET OFF FROM the Queen Elizabeth Country Park on a Tuesday at 8 a.m. I've just been dropped off by Keith in his van after leaving my car at the car park in Cocking, where I'll pick it up at the end of today's walk. The sky is overcast and there is a slight chill in the air. I have had enough time to recover after my last outing on the Downs, I ached for nearly a week after that walk from Winchester. There were times on the last couple of miles when I really thought I was going to collapse. My head was spinning, my legs felt like lead, my feet had become one big black blister and my kidneys and back ached, but other than that I felt fine after stopping at the first petrol station I came to, where I loaded up with bottles of mineral water, energy drinks and chocolate and felt a lot better after getting some sugar back into my bloodstream.

Today the birds are singing, but the sound of traffic is ringing in my ears. I pass the visitor centre and carry on past one of the many picnic areas. The place is deserted. I'm on a tarmac road that runs through the woods, and then I reach a car park where the road ends and a gravel path takes over. It's uphill for about a mile with woods and a high bank of trees either side. A couple of dog walkers pass me with a 'good morning'. In the distance the droning of the traffic on the A3

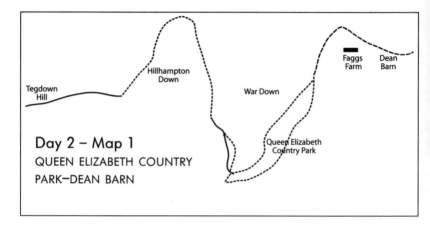

Day 2 – Map 1
QUEEN ELIZABETH COUNTRY
PARK–DEAN BARN

can be faintly heard above the birds chirping in the trees. When you reach the top of the hill, the track levels out. Off to the right there's a valley below and you can see across to Fagg's Farm. From here it's down a steep hill for about half a mile. The path is very slippery, with large bits of flint and rock, and if you were on horseback or even cycling I wouldn't chance it – I'd say now would be the time to dismount. At the bottom of the hill there's a small car park, and next to it a field with cows grazing.

Go through a gate and onto New Barn Road. Cross here and look for the signs for the South Downs Way. There's a post-box and a sign which says Halls Hill, the hill I've just come down. It can be quite confusing here because there's a wooden post with an arrow on it pointing straight on, for the South Downs Way and Hangers Way. Don't take this route, because it leads down to the village of Buriton.

Like a div, I carry straight on down the hill and end up in Buriton, the opposite way to where I should be heading. It's a very pretty, small village with a pond. I sit down on a bench facing the water, where the ducks swim towards me, hoping I'm supplying breakfast. I'm angry with myself for going the wrong way and not studying the maps I have with me. I pull them from my backpack and try to see where I've gone wrong.

Suddenly, from behind me I hear a man's voice. The ducks go wild, flap their wings and jump from the water and up on to the muddy bank. I look behind. There's an elderly man standing there dressed in a brown checked sports jacket which looks like it was made to measure, just not for him, clashing green herringbone trousers, a cloth cap, and a small kerchief tied tightly round his neck. By the looks of it Mr Hugo Boss here ain't in the fashion industry. He's more Oxfam than New York, Paris or Milan.

'Good morning, my beauties, and how are you today?'

The rear ends of the ducks shake and wag like a dog's tail as the man pulls a plastic bag from his jacket pocket, puts his hand inside and pulls a slice of bread out, which he breaks into small pieces and throws to the birds, who wait with their beaks open. The noise of squawking is deafening as they vie for the man's attention to be the first one to be fed.

'Good morning, young sir,' the man says to me in a broad Hampshire accent as he doffs his cap and sits down next to me on the damp wooden bench. 'I've not seen you around these parts before.'

I explain to him that I'm walking the South Downs Way and have somehow taken a wrong turn. He laughs and points me back in the direction I've just come from. I pull a bottle of water from my bag and take a swig, then wipe the top and offer the man some.

'No thanks, me old mate,' he says, 'I've not long had me tea and toast.' He goes on to tell me that since he retired some 20 years ago he walks from just outside Petersfield every day and comes here for an hour to feed the birds. He tells me how he worked as a labourer on the local farms for most of his life and has only ever been out of the area once, and that was during World War Two when he did his bit for the country and Churchill over in France.

'I couldn't wait to get back home, I hated every blimin' minute of it, I spent half a day in London with my pals from the regiment at the end of the war, sightseeing, and that was nearly as bad as getting shot at by the Germans, bloody people rushing about all over the place pushing and shoving, cars, trams and trolley buses trying to kill you as you cross the roads, you've got to have eyes in the back of your head. No, give me the peace and quiet of the countryside any day of the week.' He stands up and shakes my hand.

'It's been nice chatting, son, but I can't sit around chinwagging all day. I'm going off to dig over me vegetable plot and get some fresh veg for tonight's tea.'

'Will the wife cook you a nice dinner then?' I ask him.

'No, no,' he replies. 'I lost her years ago.'

'I'm sorry,' I say, cringing when the words come out of my mouth. Why am I trying to sound sincere when I didn't even know the woman? 'How did she die?'

'Oh, she ain't dead, she just fucked off to her sister's when she found out about me and another woman,' he laughs. 'I'm a bit of a rascal, I reckon I've fathered half the kids in my village,' he goes on with a wink and a twinkle in his eyes.

No wonder the dirty bastard didn't bother going further afield! He was too busy shagging!

I head back to where I went wrong. You should always carry a map and stop and study it carefully if you're not sure of the route. At the signpost back at Halls Hill I look to my right. There's a black metal farm gate with views of the cottage at Fagg's Farm. I take the track to the far right here, which leads up a slight incline to Dean Barn.

The Way is now signposted with the white acorn on a

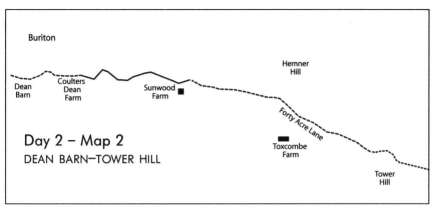

Buriton

Hemner
Hill

Dean
Barn

Coulters
Dean
Farm

Sunwood
Farm

Forty Acre Lane

Toxcombe
Farm

Tower
Hill

Day 2 – Map 2
DEAN BARN–TOWER HILL

black background. I pass some farm outbuildings. To the left there are some good views of the village of Buriton. I've already seen it, close up. The sound of a train can be heard in the distance. At the top of the hill the town of Petersfield can be seen. I carry on down the hill, which is surprisingly dry, even after all the rain this area's seen in the last few months. On the path in front of me some pheasants run out of my way as I interrupt them feeding.

When I stop and look behind I can see the masts at Butser Hill. The traffic of the A3 is behind in the distance as I pass under a line of electricity pylons, which stretch out for miles across the open countryside, and there's a humming sound from the huge cables that hang from the metal towers. I read recently that this type of electric pylon may cause cancer in people living near them, and I have noticed how our feathered friends tend to keep at a distance from them. Perhaps they know something we don't.

Go past the barn on the left at Coulters Dean Farm. Just up ahead the Way sweeps around to the left, passing the entrance and information board of the nature reserve on the right. After 100 yards the route carries on around to the right.

On the left is a footpath called Cart Track. This is marked on the map as the Milky Way, and leads back down into Buriton. For me it's uphill and on the left I can see patchwork fields. There is a steep drop below and I'm reminded of a mountain path, the sort you might see in Switzerland or anywhere in the Alps.

At the end of the track the Way goes to the left and on the right is a cottage. On the fence is a sign saying 'Private road, Ditcham Park School'. You are now on a tarmac road with views out to Sunwood Farm. This is a fairly busy road with traffic heading up and down towards the school. I can hear the kids shouting and laughing; it must be break time.

I pass the farm and turn left almost immediately. The Way then goes off to the right. Be careful here not to miss the wooden sign, like me – talking to my wife on my mobile, I carry on downhill on a tarmac road for about a mile, then have to turn back and find the sign for the South Downs Way. The track when I find it is very muddy, so I try and keep to the edges. A rabbit runs out from a hedgerow across my feet, scraping the toecap of my boots, which I've changed for today's walk. Instead of my usual walking/cycling boots, which nearly crippled me on the last walk, I'm road-testing a pair of slip-on Doc Martens dealer boots as favoured by the fashion-conscious gypsy of this land. I head towards Forty Acre Lane. I've been walking now for two hours. At the top of the lane you can look back onto Sunwood Farm and in front of you you can see the Downs above South Harting. A farmer in his tractor is busy working the fields about a mile away to my right. The South Downs Way sign now changes to green. Along here there are some good views out to Hemner Hill. The track flattens out and I see two farmers in green tractors with yellow wheels ploughing their fields. I carry on until I reach a road. The right-hand fork goes off to

ABOVE:
Nigel, Gary, Keith and I at the start of the cycle.

BELOW:
The Hungry Monk restaurant, in the village of Jevington. The restaurant claims to have invented Bannoffee Pie.

ABOVE:
The church in Jevington village.

BELOW:
On the way to Swanborough Hill.

ABOVE:
After cycling for nearly four hours, we take a well-earned
rest at Swanborough Hill.

BELOW:
Gary and me. I've never felt so happy.

ABOVE:
The hills seemed to go on forever. At least we were going
down this one on the cycle.

BELOW:
A signpost typical of those along the South Downs Way. This
one is at the bottom of Newbarn Road, near Buriton.

ABOVE:
The view above Littleton Farm.

BELOW:
I've been walking for four hours, and I'm about to stop just below the radio masts near Bignor Hill and take in the views of Chichester and the sea.

ABOVE:
Notice the lack of trees on this stretch of the Way, between Southease village and Alfriston.

BELOW:
One of the dew ponds found on the Downs, originally used to water sheep and cattle. This one is at Ditchling Beacon.

ABOVE:
Jack and Jill, the windmills above Clayton.

BELOW:
The view above the Seven Sisters Country Park, where the
River Cuckmere runs into the sea.

ABOVE:
The Birling Gap. In the background are the Seven Sisters.

BELOW:
The last remaining cottages at the Birling Gap. The sea has
eroded this stretch of
coastline significantly.

Foxcombe Farm and to the left the road leads to Torberry Hill. I am now in West Sussex, having just crossed from the county of Hampshire at the boundary at One Hundred Acres, which is just east of Sunwood Farm. The unmarked county boundary was once the official end of the South Downs Way until it was extended to Winchester in 1989.

I carry on down Forty Acre Lane, a muddy flint track which runs in between a row of trees. Above me on Tower Hill are some ruins that look like a Stonehenge-type of structure.

At the end of Forty Acre Lane, there is a small car park. I come out there and go across the B2146 road, which runs between South Harting and Uppark County House, built in the 1690s and now owned by the National Trust; it was rebuilt after a fire in 1989. Continue up a single chalk track through some woods. The track is uphill and the ground rises rapidly to reveal views of the green copper steeple of South Harting church. The track carries on for another mile, with traffic down below to the right. The sound of struggling engines and gears changing means cars are struggling to get up the steep hill, where you're heading on foot. At the top of the track another road, the B2141, runs in front of you. Cross the road and you are now out onto the open spaces of

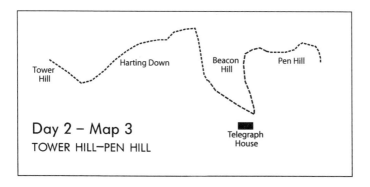

Day 2 – Map 3
TOWER HILL–PEN HILL

Harting Down. There's a car park off to the right. Here there are some panoramic views. Today the sun is out and it's quite warm, with butterflies and wasps catching the last sunshine of the summer, even though it's now October.

A group of around 50 school children pass me by with their teacher as I head through a wooden gate surrounded by bushes. I am heading in the direction of Beacon Hill. What look like either swallows or swifts fly and dive in the clear skies above. I can see the mast at Butser Hill. It has taken me two and a half hours to get this far. The Downs really open out at this point. There are rolling green hills and beautiful English countryside. From here you can see the North Downs out towards Hogsback in Surrey, and way out into the distance deep into the heart of the Hampshire countryside towards Basingstoke.

Below me are the villages of South and East Harting and Elstead. It's very peaceful, though every now and then a cock pheasant lets out a screech. If you want to chill out for a few hours or for the day, then this is the place. I've only seen two people walking since I left Queen Elizabeth Country Park. A day up here should be on prescription from your GP; this is stress-free. And remember to bring a video camera. Half a mile away in the distance someone on horseback gallops across the open spaces and then stops, no doubt to take in the superb views.

I can hear the sounds of shotguns popping and the crack of a high-powered rifle. Smoke rises from farms down below. A field a couple of miles away has bales of hay spread over it. In the field next door there must be 200 sheep grazing. At the bottom of Beacon Hill there is a metal water trough and a wooden signpost with fingers sending you in different directions: Buriton, East Harting, Beacon Hill, Hooksway and Compton. The base of the signpost is set in flint stone.

From here you can go two ways, following the South Downs Way. One route is straight up and over Beacon Hill, while the other goes along the valley at Bramshott towards Telegraph House.

I've been walking for three hours now and I've chosen the route up the side of Beacon Hill. Chalk steps cut into the hillside make it an easier climb. I stop halfway and regain my breath. This is hard work – perhaps I should have taken the slightly easier route through Bramshott Valley. I can see where rabbits have been burrowing into the hillside and not finished. They probably thought, 'Fuck it, I'm not going to live this high up and have to hop up here to get home,' and abandoned the project. When you reach the top, there's a wooden gate. Be careful passing through, there's a wooden toe board, so don't trip up and tumble back down where it's taken you 20 minutes to come from.

The views up here are magnificent in all directions. You can see across to Chichester and the sea beyond that, and all of South Harting behind. Although the path is a bit of a climb, it is the shortest way for walkers. There's no way you could cycle to the very top of Beacon Hill. At the top there's a metal compass with an inscription that reads: 'Harting Down was given to the National Trust in memory of Nicholas Bogwell aged 75, who tragically died on 5 May 1987'. As I stop to read the distances engraved on the compass – Winchester 30 miles, Selsey Bill 17 miles, Chichester 9 miles, Goodwood Racecourse 7 miles, Farnham 18 miles, Hogsback Guildford 20 miles, Butser Hill 6 miles – the sound of gunfire seems to get closer. I make my way down the other side of the hill, towards the bottom of Pen Hill. Mill Pond Bottom is on my right. I can remember standing down here when me, Keith, Gary and Nigel cycled this part of the Downs, arguing about which way to go.

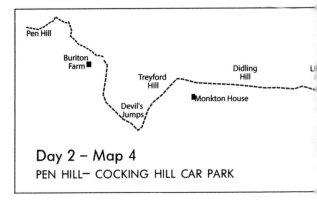

Day 2 – Map 4
PEN HILL– COCKING HILL CAR PARK

I follow the South Downs Way sign and head up Pen Hill. The sound of rifles cracks away. It's definitely getting closer. I stop and look behind me. The screech of a pheasant breaks the silence. I stand dead still. I check nothing's at my back, then move off up the hill again. I feel as if someone's watching me. At the top of Pen Hill you have views down onto Buriton Farm, and to the left there are views out towards Elstead and Treyford. Get your camera out, because the scenery here is something else.

I make my way downhill now towards the wooded area of Mount Sinai. I remember climbing in the opposite direction when we were cycling towards Winchester and we stopped halfway, absolutely knackered. I stop and take off my rucksack to get a picture of Buriton Farm, when suddenly through the trees comes a camouflaged army Land Rover. Two men jump out and leap quickly into some bushes, where they lie flat. At the same time a helicopter comes over from the direction of Beacon Hill and lands in the field to my right. It's only on the ground for seconds before it takes off again. The two men jump to their feet, scramble back into their motor and are off up Pen Hill. I snap a picture of the helicopter as it rises up and heads off in the direction of

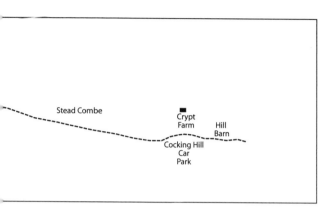

Midhurst. Someone's playing war games, or an extravagant game of paintballing.

Now the Way goes onto a single muddy footpath, which is very wet. I've been walking now for three and a half hours. My feet are beginning to ache. As I follow the wooden signposts, the gunfire starts up again but it is now well behind me and it seems that Rambo and his mates are moving away in the opposite direction to me.

At the end of the track the South Downs Way goes to the left. If you were to turn right the flint farm track would take you down to Buriton Farm with its barn and cottage. When you turn left, almost immediately, after 40 yards, the Way takes a right turn and from here it's uphill, past a disused chalk pit. Carry on through the woods and past a gate with a signpost that reads 'Westand Estate – Private No Right Of Way'. Philliswood Wood is down on the right. On the left you come to a small clearing with a tiny memorial stone for Hauptman, Joseph Oesterman, a German pilot killed in 1940 during World War Two. I stop and take a photo. I feel sorry for the man, but if he had not been shot down how many people would he have killed with his bombs? Just up ahead there is a green wooden sign with a white acorn that sends you around to the left. After about 400 yards there is a series of five mounds called the Devil's Jumps. These can be reached for a closer view by a small path that runs off the main trail.

On the left is a footpath that runs off the Way down towards another disused pit at Treyford Hill. I am now walking on a gravelly surface, on a track wide enough to take a vehicle, and on the right is a 10ft-high chain link fence topped with barbed wire. Behind this are the grounds of Monkton House. I carry on for another couple of miles with woods either side and then the path opens out with fields on both sides. There are hundreds of sheep grazing in the sun, which is quite warming on my face. Off to the right I can see the ground stands of Goodwood Racecourse and out to the left are views of Midhurst and Cocking. It's nice to be out in the open after the long walk through the woods. The ground rises gently here towards Didling Hill, which is off to the left. Along this stretch there are sheep, sheep and more sheep behind wire fencing. I've seen no one since Harting Down.

The views out towards Surrey are spectacular. A farmer in his blue tractor is busy ploughing the fields and a flock of birds follows, looking for a juicy worm for their lunch. The ground is very dry. I make my way downhill and then back up. On the left is a wooden tower about 30ft high. It looks like a machine-gun tower that would be found in a prisoner-of-war camp, but it's probably used for bird watching or shooting. It doesn't look too clever and seems to be in need of a few more nails and a coat of creosote. It wouldn't hold my weight. On the right is a ladder going up a tree with a platform used for deer or pheasant shooting. It also looks very cheaply made, and I wouldn't want to put it to the test. In the distance coming towards me are two people on horseback. When we pass, I see that they are two very pretty girls, one with long blonde hair and the other with long dark hair. They both say 'hello' and smile. They're the best thing I've seen all day.

I am now at Linch Ball and there's a farmer sitting down with his back resting on the front wheel of his tractor reading *The Sun*. He's had a hard day. I pass Stead Combe on the left and on my right are the trees of Linch Ball Wood, which seems to run for miles. Not far now. There are some good views of Goodwood and out to Chichester. I pass a sign for the Way, and a galvanised metal water tank. From here it's downhill. I can see Hill Barn, which is on the other side of the A286 road and on the left at the bottom is Crypt Farm.

I've been walking for five hours now and my feet are killing me again. It's back to the drawing board where the correct footwear is concerned. The chalk and granite stone beneath my boots digs into the soles, and every step is now painful. A large group of pheasants flies up into the air as I approach. Some get tangled in the hedge as they escape on foot. There are good views in all directions. The sun is shining and there's no wind. I'm surprised there are no hot air balloons out today, because usually along this stretch of the Downs you can look out towards Petworth and Guildford and see up to a dozen balloons gently floating over the Sussex and Surrey countryside.

As I approach Crypt Farm, a walker comes off a footpath that runs across the South Downs Way and carries on in the direction of Cocking. He's dressed in full hiking gear, with the best boots, red socks tucked into his waterproof trousers and a red fleece top, a nylon waterproof rucksack on his back and a map in hand. He beats me in the countryside fashion stakes and doesn't give me a hello or a second look, obviously not taking me very seriously. He's probably thinking, 'Look at that tramp dressed in green army combat trousers and black DMs'. There is a bit of fashion snobbery on the Downs.

It takes me five hours and ten minutes to complete the walk and I celebrate with the remains of my drinking water and the last of my egg-salad sandwiches. I've done 13 and a half miles today. Perhaps an investment in some good walking boots will help me get to Eastbourne with my feet intact and blister-free.

I'm back in the car park where I dropped my car off at seven that morning. From here Keith drove me to the Queen Elizabeth Country Park, where I set off. I get into the car, pull off my boots and let out a huge sigh of relief. As I start up the engine, my mobile phone rings. It's Keith. 'Kingy, how ya doing?' he asks.

'Fine, Keith,' I reply. 'I've just finished.' I take a huge gulp of water and drive with bare feet out of the car park and head for home, happy that day two of the walk is out of the way.

TOURIST INFORMATION
Petersfield Tel: 01730 68829

LOCAL AMENITIES
Queen Elizabeth Country Park, visitors' centre (café and toilets)
Butser Hill information centre (café and toilets)

TAXIS
As there is no railway station along this part of the Way, the nearest being at Petersfield or Chichester, besides your own transport or buses the only alternative is to take a taxi.

1 4 U Cars, Petersfield Tel: 01730 231347
5 Ways Cars, Buriton Tel: 01730 260442
A. J. Connect, Waterlooville Tel: 02392 233770
Andicars, Waterlooville Tel: 02392 350350

BUSES

The number 60 bus runs from just outside the car park at Cocking on the A286. It goes to Chichester and onto Bognor on the far side of the road, and on the near side it goes to Midhurst and onto Guildford.

LOCAL PLACES OF INTEREST

Uppark House, 17th- or 18th-century museum and gardens

The Weald and Downland open-air museum at Singleton

West Dean Gardens at Singleton

Fishbourne Roman Palace, near Chichester

Royal Military Police Museum, Roussillon Barracks, Chichester

Goodwood House and Racecourse

The Walk – Day Three

COCKING HILL CAR PARK–AMBERLEY

IT'S FRIDAY 6 OCTOBER, and the sun is out. The weather is bright and dry with a clear blue sky and no wind. I'm walking from the car park at the bottom of Cocking Hill to Amberley. I cross the A286 onto the Way, a gravel track here. A 6ft-high bramble hedge runs along the side of the path to Hillbarn Farm. There is a chalk pit up on a hill to the left.

The path rises in a long, slow incline. Outside one of the farm buildings, green plastic sheeting covers huge piles of bales of hay. At the farm there are barns and outbuildings and to the right there is a timber yard with stacks of seasoned timber stacked neatly. Hanging from a fence on the left is a sign for the Bluebell Inn, which reads 'Food, beer and beds two minutes away'. There is also a tap here with drinking water.

I carry on past two cottages with orange paint around their window frames, and when I look back towards Crypt Farm I see that quite a few houses have the same colour of paintwork. Someone must have bought a cheap job lot of this shitty coloured paint. The bright colour of the woodwork indicates that the property belongs to the Cowdray Estate. What cheapskates! When I lived in London, though, my next-door neighbour had his house painted in a similar colour.

I am now on a tarmac track. The road splits here. The

right-hand fork is the one to take, and the lane now becomes chalk. Up ahead is Charlton Forest. There's a green sign with a white acorn on it. Behind is a chalk path that leads up from Middlefield Lane to Cocking Down. Tucked away in the woods are two cottages at Warren Bottom and Stubbs Copse. A trail of smoke rises from one of the chimneys and evaporates into the clear blue sky as I climb higher. The sound of the traffic on the A286 is fading, but you can still see the motors speeding along. From here they are the size of dinky cars, and the sound of birds chirping and singing soon replaces the sound of roaring engines.

The farm at Hill Barn is well below me now as I head off towards Grafton Down. Two people on horseback nod and wish me a good morning as they gallop past. I'm still heading uphill and a slight breeze is now blowing. The ground now becomes a bit muddier – it looks like a tractor or mountain bike with huge tyres has turned the path over. As you go through the woods, the sun disappears and once out of the direct sunlight you notice a chill in the air. On the left is a wooden gate and as you look into the field, you can see one of those wooden platforms used for deer shooting or bird watching. This one, like the others I've seen, doesn't look too safe. The path here is a bed of fallen leaves, which help to

Day 3 – Map 1
COCKING HILL CAR PARK–LITTLETON FARM

keep the trail dry. Almost opposite the wooden structure next to the path is a triangular fence which shields a stone. It looks like the headstone of a grave. Apparently this stone dates from around 1500 BC and marks the site of cremations. Carry on past this and head towards Graffham Down, where the Way opens up.

I've been walking for an hour now and there are good views to the left over Heyshott. On the right is open land filled with thistles and stinging nettles. The ground is very dry with the odd patch of grass growing in between the flint. Running parallel to the South Downs Way and cutting in from the right is a track called the Board Walk. On a wooden gate is a sign which reads 'The Grafton Downs Trust (GDT) Reservation'. This downland is under the management of the GDT with the aim of preserving the original downland turf and conserving the many plants, butterflies and orchids that it supports.

To the left, through the gaps in the trees, I can pick out two cottages in among the patchwork quilt of different coloured fields and can see the road between Graffam and East Lavington, with the soundless movement of cars creeping along.

I pass through a tunnel of bushes and trees, which bend

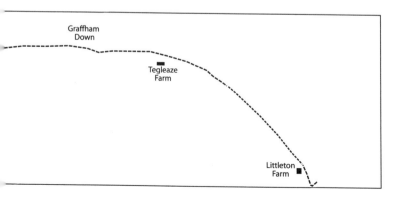

down almost to head height, now heading uphill. On the right is an old, solid wooden signpost bearing inscriptions which read 'Sylvia Helen Laura Barkworth died 18 July 1983, 82 years old' and 'Edmond Barkworth 1906–97'. The signs point in the direction of East Dean, East Lavington, Graffham and Upwaltham.

I carry straight on here until I reach the top of a small hill. From here I can see out towards Chanctonbury Ring. The Hogs Back and the North Downs are way out in the distance to my left. Down below I can see the top of Seaford College, where that famous football hooligan turned author and punk singer Chris 'Chubby' Henderson once attended. So much for the working-class roots he once sang about. Next to it is Woolavington Down.

The Way ascends here, and the views behind are spectacular. Out to the left you can see to the bottom of the Downs, with the white canopies of trailers being towed around the fields by blue tractors. Someone has been hard at work loading these with freshly dug cabbages, potatoes, sprouts or whatever it is they grow. When you reach the top of the hill there are good views down below onto the town at Petworth. Petworth House and its surrounding parkland can be clearly seen, and I'm reminded of Richmond Park in London. Up here there is also a wooden signpost set in flint which points towards Duncton to the north, and to East Dean to the south. The words '1922–72 Cowdray Hunt' are inscribed into the weathered timber, and Jim has left his mark by telling the world how much he loves Sally, whoever Jim is (or was) when he's at home.

Carry on following the signs for the South Downs Way, which along this stretch is very well marked. I'm walking along a muddy farm track, which goes into some woods at the end. From here you can see the radio masts just off Bignor

Hill and, halfway across a ploughed field to the left, a group of houses and farm buildings called Dog Kennel Cottages. There's a public phone box here. At the bottom of the ploughed field there's a wooden gate. I carry on downhill towards another wooden bridle gate, go through this and head down the lane I come out into. At the bottom of it, about 200 yards along, is Littleton Farm. As you pass here some dogs might well come out barking. There are two of them and you'll hear them before you see them. It's guaranteed they'll hear you – I promise. You have been warned.

The A285 road is now in front of me. The South Downs Way is almost directly facing me across the other side of the road. The road here is very fast and fairly busy so use the utmost care when crossing. Once across, follow the sign for the South Downs Way. On the right is a small pond (or a large puddle), full of dirty, black silage-filled water and it stinks. Up on the hills to the left is Rarm Hill. There's a fire-break cut in the trees; in quite a few places along the Way you can see an alleyway of felled trees. The top of Butser Hill, looking down onto the A3 and the Queen Elizabeth Country Park, is a good example of forest management and fire-breaks.

Up a steep hill the lane forks. Take the right-hand path. On the left is Scotcher's Bottom. The path is very chalky and if it's wet extra care should be taken as it's very slippery underfoot. At a hay field on the left the ground flattens out. I've been walking for just over three hours and today my feet have stood up remarkably to the rigours of the walk, no blisters yet, touch wood. (I tap my head.) The ground rises again for 300 yards or more. There's a wooden bench on the left and a lane off to the right. It's poorly signposted here, so I carry straight on. The sun's still shining and there's only a

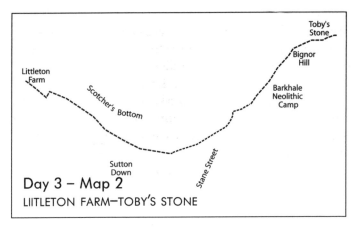

slight breeze.

I stop and try to use my mobile phone, but I can't get a signal here for some reason. I don't believe it, I'm standing high up on the Sussex Downs and I can't get a fucking signal. I've got to be nearer a poxy satellite than if I was in one of the towns 600ft below. Still, that's modern technology for you. Further along the track are two aerials. I don't know if they are phone masts or not, but they don't make any difference to my fucking phone.

I follow the path along and come to a wooden gate. Here I stop and take in the views. Out to my right I can get a clear view of the sea as far as the Isle of Wight, while to my left there's Butlins holiday centre at Bognor, with its huge white Millennium Dome-type canopy and further along the spire of Chichester Cathedral. The scenery is amazing.

A sign hanging on the gate tells me that this part of the Downs is the Slindon Estate, part of the National Trust. I go through a field with hundreds of sheep grazing peacefully. They don't give me a second look, preferring to munch away. The path through the field is about half a mile long. The sea out on the right seems to go on for miles. You can see ships and boats of all sizes bobbing up and down on the blue-grey ocean. Smoke from bonfires down below gets lost as it rises in the hazy sunshine. The coastline stretches out towards Littlehampton, Shoreham and Brighton. I stop for ten minutes and sit on the grass to take in the views and have a sandwich and a drink. I've learnt from my first couple of walks out on these downs that rest and liquid refreshment are very important.

Soon I get myself together and head towards a bridle gate. Just below it on the left I see what appears to be a hare or a rabbit. It doesn't seem bothered that I'm coming in its direction, and as I get closer I can see why – the small fluffy creature is in fact a tree stump. That reminds me, I must get my eyes tested.

Once through the gate at the other end of the field the path joins Stane Street, which was once a Roman road that was constructed to connect Chichester with London. This route was used to carry corn, iron and trade goods and its raised embankment makes it very distinctive. It was reserved for use by official messengers, and the Roman army for manoeuvres. Other people used the lower path, or slow lane. Nearby at Cumber Farm there is a National Trust camping bar with water and toilets available to the public. I stop and speak to a man who's stopped on the other side of the gate. He tells me that he's ridden from Findon, which is over near Worthing, and plans finishing his ride at Cocking. All in all it's about a 15-mile ride. He complains that his bum is a bit sore and fiddles with his cycling shorts. Why he thought I'd want to know that I don't know. I ask him if his problem was caused by his boyfriend the night before or by cycling, but he doesn't seem to have my sense of humour and cycles off shaking his head and mumbling something about only trying to be friendly.

Bignor Hill car park comes into view, and what looks like two kestrels float in the air, gliding on the thermals. I think they are kestrels, anyway, although they could well be buzzards. Apparently buzzards are quite common in the south of England, and whereas a kestrel will lunch on a mouse or vole, a buzzard might easily swoop down and take off with a lamb or even a small dog gripped in its beak or razor-sharp claws.

In the car park there is a signpost pointing to London and various other places. The National Trust owns over 3,500 acres here, which were left to it in the 1950s.

At the bottom of the Downs, near the village of Bignor, is a Roman villa, which is thought to date from about AD 70 and is well worth a visit. The views from up here are something else and stretch far out in front of me, and I can even see a white building above the town of Ewhurst, which is on the Surrey part of the North Downs. I can also see the brick tower at Leith Hill and just further along the North Downs Box Hill, near Dorking and Marjory Hill, which is just outside Reigate, can be viewed. The North and South Downs are separated by a 22-mile gap of weald land.

Just south of the car park, going in the direction of Eartham Woods, is the Barkhale Neolithic Camp, which, although plough-damaged, has 13 separate entrances and was thought to have been used as a tribal meeting place where animals were ritually slaughtered and where social and religious festivals took place – a sort of ancient community centre without bingo. I can imagine the Romans coming along Stane Street and hopping off their chariots to stretch their legs and have a piss. A vehicle comes towards me as I head out of the car park. Could this be the ghost of Julius Caesar? No, not in a grey BT van, that's for sure.

From the car park you head towards the top of Bignor Hill,

and halfway along the track you can get good views of Arundel. Out towards Worthing and Shoreham you can see the traffic going along the top of Bury Hill in the distance. Eartham Woods is out to your right. At the top of the hill, which is about half a mile from the car park, there are some splendid views. To your left are vistas of Pulborough and Storrington. Further out you can see the hills of the North Downs that stretch out towards Oxted, Sevenoaks and down into Kent. You can see the planes climbing into the air as they take off from Gatwick Airport. The Downs here are very open and you have a great feeling of space. There are sheep grazing on the steep slopes and a farmer out towards West Burton Hill is ploughing his fields. Flocks of white seagulls follow him as his tractor turns over the earth.

I begin to go downhill from here. Toby's Stone is on the left. It looks like a broken gravestone. One part has an inscription that reads 'James Wentworth Fitzwilliam "Toby", once secretary of the local hunt'. The stone is in the shape of a horse-mounting block. I spot another walker about half a mile in front of me and follow him downhill past open fields with sheep grazing. The ground is very dry. Surprising really with all the rain we've had recently. The path zigzags down a hard flint trail. Below is a barn with a green roof. There are two other outbuildings and in a field is a huge bull with a metal ring through his nose. I stop and he looks at me, standing there almost daring me to climb the fence and come into the field with him. Not bloody likely, mate, I ain't that daft. I bid him good day and carry on my way. Outside one of the buildings there was a huge 2ft-deep muddy puddle the last time we passed here on our bikes. Today there's nothing. The mud and puddle have disappeared.

From here it's uphill towards Bury Hill. Farm vehicles have been along here and cut into the trail and a verge of grass has

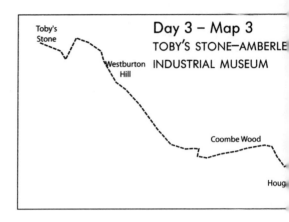

Day 3 – Map 3
TOBY'S STONE–AMBERLE
INDUSTRIAL MUSEUM

Toby's
Stone

Westburton
Hill

Coombe Wood

Houg

grown in between the ruts. Carry on for a couple of miles and Houghton Forest and Kings Buildings are off to the left. If you are cycling along this stretch, be very careful. Some of the tracks left by vehicles can be very deep. I speak from experience – I fell arse-over-tit here when I was cycling. There's nothing worse than lying upside down in a gorse bush with the sound of laughter ringing in your ears from fellow travellers. I've not got far to go now. I've been walking for five hours. The Way levels out and in front of you, down in the valley, are the villages of Houghton and Amberley. You can now see the car park to your right at the top of Bury Hill. It's a good place to get a drink or something to eat. There's a van that serves hot and cold drinks, sandwiches and snacks. It's a great place to stop and rest. There are toilets and a public phone box, and at weekends, if you are a motorbike fan, there are bikes of all ages and makes. People come from everywhere to chat and pose on their machines; it's a biker's paradise.

In front of you is the A29. Turn right, then follow the trail, and, after about 50 yards, opposite you is the South Downs Way. Carry on down a wide chalk lane. From here you can see the industrial museum and railway station down in

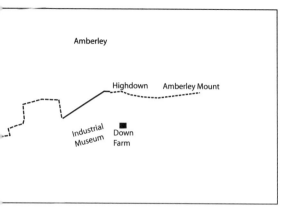

Amberley

Highdown   Amberley Mount

Industrial
Museum

Down
Farm

Amberley, and even where the Way continues, on the other side of the village and off and up towards Downs Farm and Amberley Mount. Civilisation doesn't look that far away. My feet are aching. They could do with a rest. I've tried trainers today, but I'm going to have to invest in a good pair of proper walking boots.

The noise of the traffic fades as I leave the road behind me. On the left is Coombe Wood and to the right are freshly ploughed fields which have an amazing, fresh country smell to them. Up here you can get some good views of the River Arun in front, with Bury church on the right. The brick double bridge that crosses the river at Houghton, near Amberley, is in the distance,

From here there are two possible ways to go. I want to end my walk at Amberley Railway Station car park, so instead of following the signs for the South Downs Way I turn right onto the tarmac road that runs down past Houghton Farm. At the end I turn left along the busy B2139, past St Nicholas's church where there is a phone box at the brick bridge which spans the River Arun. I head past the Boathouse Restaurant in Amberley, where there is a tea-room next to the river. You can stop and relax, or if you're feeling energetic maybe hire a rowing boat. This is a good place to start or end a walk on the Downs.

I go under the railway bridge and turn right into the car park. There's a post box and public phone box here, but be careful about parking because the car park belongs to the Industrial Museum, so make sure you don't get a penalty ticket, and check the times they lock the gates.

The railway station is served by trains to and from London and down to the south coast. You can also catch a bus from here to Storrington and there is a taxi company called Castle Cars who advertise on a noticeboard at the entrance to the museum. All in all, the walk has taken me six hours. My feet have held up well today and the weather was superb. It's been a really enjoyable day's walking.

TAXIS
Bognor Taxis Tel: 01243 828282
Castle Cars Amberley Tel: 0800 332211
Eastbourne Taxis, Midhurst Tel: 01730 816895

RAIL
Amberley station
Pulborough station

BUS
84 from Bury Hill

TOURIST INFORMATION
Chichester Tel: 01243 775888
Bognor Regis Tel: 01243 823140
Fontwell Tel: 01243 543269

YOUTH HOSTELS AND OTHER ACCOMMODATION

Arundel Youth Hostel Tel: 01903 882204

Duncton Mill, B & B* Duncton Hill

Manor Farm, B & B*, Beachwood Lane, Duncton Hill,

The Old Railway Station, North Petworth, converted railway carriages Tel: 01798 342346

Badgers Restaurant and Bar (accommodation available), Petworth Tel: 01798 342651

Gumber Farm campsite, Bignor Hill Tel: 01243 814484

LOCAL PLACES OF INTEREST

Petworth House and Park

Roman Villa at Bignor

Amberley Industrial Museum

Amberley Castle

Parham House and gardens

Arundel Castle

* Phone numbers not available

The Walk – Day Four

AMBERLEY–UPPER BEEDING

IT'S A GREY, OVERCAST morning. My wife Mandy has dropped me off and I'm waiting in the car park of the Industrial Museum at Amberley, right next door to the railway station. I'm expecting to meet my friend Martin Knight and his mate Paul, who are joining me here today, at 10 a.m. Martin Knight is on a bit of a health kick. He's recently gone on a diet and is increasing his exercise, so what better way to see how he's doing than a 13-mile walk? From our recent conversations I know he's not looking forward to it. Paul, on the other hand, is an ex-squaddie who enjoys the outdoor life. Both are keen ornithologists, so a day out in the fresh air, birdwatching in the countryside while walking, will be right up their street.

I've purchased some brand-new walking boots and thick walking socks so I'm ready to put them to the test. My phone goes. It's Martin – they are both in Paul's wife's car, but they're running late just for a change and somehow seem to have got lost. 'Still, we shouldn't be long,' he tells me. Half an hour later Lorna drives Martin and Paul into the car park.

By 11 a.m. we've all had our photos taken by the girls and we're off. We go out of the car park and turn right past the Industrial Museum. We follow the footpath that runs parallel with a field where there are some donkeys grazing. We then

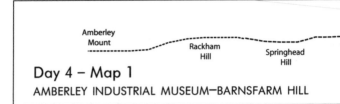

Amberley
Mount

Rackham
Hill

Springhead
Hill

Day 4 – Map 1
AMBERLEY INDUSTRIAL MUSEUM–BARNSFARM HILL

cross the B2139 road and follow the signs for the South Downs Way, which leads us up a lane called High Tutterns. The Way quickly rises with good views to your right of Amberley Castle, where the castle flag flutters wildly in the wind. A big mansion house with a red-tiled roof called High Down comes up in front of us. The Way turns right here and heads towards Downs Farm. Within 100 yards the Way goes off to the left, uphill and through some trees. We pass through a wooden gate with open fields to both sides of us, on a very muddy track. Then we go through a metal gate and head up towards Amberley Mount. There are cows feeding through a metal fence and a couple of the young calves have managed to squeeze through and are getting the pick of the feed scattered by the high winds, which are getting up by the minute.

Suddenly the heavens open and rain pours from the now-black skies. I knew rain was forecast, but didn't realise it would be this heavy. Should we carry on? We reach the top of Rackham Hill and the winds are very strong. It has also started raining even harder now, so it's off with the rucksack and out with my plastic poncho. The gusts are so strong I'm having trouble getting it on, that's how much the wind has got up in the last few minutes. Martin and Paul manage to get their wet weather gear on, so they are sorted, but I'm not. A gust of wind rips my poncho in two as I pull it over my head. I've now got a piece in each hand, and I'm not holding

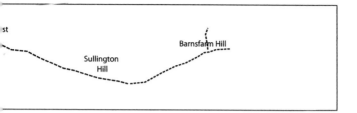

st

Barnsfarm Hill

Sullington
Hill

that very long before the wind sends it flying up into the air and across the Downs, the pieces of white plastic blowing away like two kites. The rain begins to fall even harder and is being driven into our faces by the howling wind. After five minutes I'm soaked through. I only have on a sweatshirt and a pair of tracksuit bottoms. Talk about not coming prepared. We've only covered about three miles and it looks as though I've just stepped out of the shower with my clothes on. The bitterly wet wind is blowing like a gale. Martin pulls the cord on the hood of his waterproof jacket tighter then wipes the rain from his glasses. Paul pulls up his collar, and I take off my baseball cap and shake the rain off it. My beige top is now dark brown, soaked through with this poxy rain.

Down below us, through the monsoon, we can just make out the village of Rackham. A mate of mine, a London cab driver who does this route regularly, reckons there's a blinding pub in Rackham called the Sportsman, the only one in the village. Him and a couple of his mates were out cycling from Winchester to Eastbourne one day when they ran out of daylight. They stopped for a pint and something to eat and resigned themselves to sleeping rough or carrying on their journey until they finished, which is a pretty dangerous thing to do in the dark. The governor of the pub overheard them talking about their predicament and offered the boys his conservatory in which to sleep, which they gratefully accepted. Next morning before they left, the owner's wife did them a full breakfast after first letting each one have a wash and brush up.

Further along from Rackham is Parham House and Park. The Way levels out here, but with the rain it is turning very muddy. We're now heading towards Springhead Hill. I'm soaked through, but at least my socks and boots are holding up to the weather. We pass the car park at the bottom of Kithurst Hill, which has a white painted signpost and an information board that describes the surrounding area. Down below to the right, through the mist and rain we can just make out Springhead Farm. To the left a public footpath and bridleway lead off towards Lee Farm. We've been walking for about one and a half hours and Paul takes out a silver hip flask filled with brandy. We all take a swig and the brandy instantly warms me up. We chat about his days in the army and the survival training he's done in the past. He tells me that even on his days off he'd think nothing of heading off to the mountains in Wales and living off the land for a while.

Martin seems to be all right, although his wet-weather gear is letting in some rain. The rain is so heavy, it's seeping in through his collar and cuffs and he complains of having a stomach-ache. We're going downhill now and we come to the car park at Chantry Post.

In the distance is Sullington Hill, but little else can be seen due to the driving rain and mist, which is rising from the ploughed fields. We keep to the right-hand side of the car park and follow the Way over a metal cattle grid. Bike or horse riders would have to dismount here and go through the metal gate next to the grid. A bit further along is a similar set-up. We stop and shelter at a barn just to get out of the rain for a few minutes and have another shot of brandy and a Mars Bar. What a combination! We speak to two other people who have also taken up refuge from the inclement weather and are walking towards Winchester. After a few minutes we're back out in the rain, as we agree it's best to keep going and get this walk over as quickly as possible. Martin wipes the rain from his goggles and stops to pull his hood tighter. He rubs his side and says he doesn't know if he has a stitch from walking or if he's got gut-ache. He grimaces and rubs his wet hands on his belly.

'Are you alright, Mart?' I ask him. 'Do you want to stop for a few minutes?'

He says he's OK, but might have to stop soon for a dump.

We're heading towards Barnsfarm Hill now. The Way is quite flat along this part and it is here that we see a wooden sign with two arrows. Follow these for the alternative route so that you miss the busy A24. The detour is two miles long and takes you down past Home Farm Cottages, through Washington village and back onto the South Downs Way at the car park at Elborne House. We decide to take the old route and head towards Highdown Hill. Here you find an odd-looking building made of concrete and metal surrounded by a barbed-wire fence. No, it's not something from a episode of *Dr Who*; this strange-looking piece of architecture which looks so out of place up here is in fact a gunport or turret, part of Britain's defences during World War Two.

Martin decides he needs to have a shit and quick, so off he goes in a flash to have a dump behind the Tardis. He must be busting as he undoes his trousers while still running. I've never seen his little legs move so quickly. Always take toilet paper with you on a long walk in the country. Don't rely on stinging nettles, as they leave a rash. Ask Martin – he learnt the hard way!

The path goes past a radio mast and begins to drop quite rapidly. The heavens are still chucking it down and we've

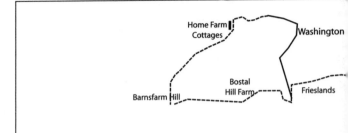

Day 4 – Map 2
BARNSFARM HILL–NEW HILL BARN

been walking for nearly three hours. We stop under some trees, which shelter us from the driving rain, to have a drink and decide to carry on. The village of Washington is only ten minutes' walk away, but we agree to carry on up to Upper Beeding, which we estimate will take us an hour to reach, so off we go again.

We are now on a tarmac road just wide enough for a vehicle, heading downhill, and the overhang of trees is giving us a break from the rain. We pass Bostal Hill Farm, where there is a water tap – no need to fill up today. I still have a full bottle in my backpack.

The A24 road is less than 200 yards away and the noise of the traffic as it thunders along this busy road can be clearly heard. It's a dual carriageway both sides of a 10ft strip of grass. We cross and follow the signs for the Way, which along this stretch is very well marked.

The route goes through a car park with an information board at the entrance, then takes you steadily uphill and past

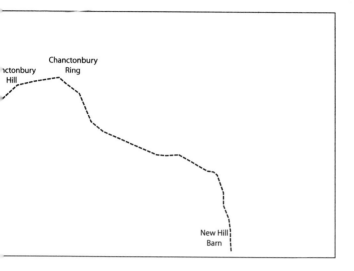

Chanctonbury
Ring

nctonbury
Hill

New Hill
Barn

a gas sub-board station. We stop and Martin falls to the floor, complaining of cramp and saying that the tops of his legs are rubbing and sore. We ask him if he wants to call it a day, but to our surprise he gets back up and carries on. The ground is fairly firm here, wide enough to take a vehicle. The rain is belting across the Downs, blown by a gale-force wind. After walking uphill for half an hour, the path levels out. The Way swings off to the left, with another track going right. It is not very well signposted here.

Back on route there's an artificial dew pond on the left, which was originally constructed around 1870. An information board near the entrance gives more details. We pass over a cattle grid next to a bridle gate and Chanctonbury Ring comes up on the left. We can just make out the ring of beech trees through the wind, and the rain and mist gives the area the feel of a horror movie. You expect to hear the screams of unsuspecting walkers being carried off by a cloaked bloodsucker or a hairy werewolf. The ring of trees were planted, it is said, by a young Charles Goring of nearby Wiston in 1760. For months he carried water uphill in a bottle to aid the growth of the trees. When some of them were blown over during the storm of 1987, interesting Iron Age and Roman sites were discovered and successfully excavated before new trees were planted. We've planned to meet two friends here, Terry and Jim, who are going to join us on the last leg of the walk, and although we are in contact with them by mobile phone, the weather is so bad that we can't see one another. Visibility is down to less than 10ft. They've parked their car and come looking for us but eventually give up and go back to their car. We tell them on the phone to sound the horn, and although we can hear them we have no idea which direction the sound is coming from. If we could only find them, the plan is that if they don't want to walk in this weather then Martin can jump in their car and meet us at the end.

But we all decide to carry on and head towards the town of Steyning. We cross a multi-path and bridleway junction near Chalkpit Walk. Jim and Terry phone and tell us they are back up on the Downs looking for us. Martin now wants to go off on his own and look for them. He has finally had enough and has complained a few times about his legs being stiff and sore. He plonks himself down on the ground again. He's wet through and cold. We talk him out of going off on his own, since he could quite easily get lost in these conditions. A man on a mountain bike comes along and jokes that he is not the only mad one in the world. We stop and chat for a few minutes and he tells us he saw Terry and Jim getting back into their car about two miles away in the car park at Chanctonbury Ring. We carry on, with Martin mumbling to himself.

The path is flat here but in places the rain is forming into very large puddles. We pass the trees of Lion Woods. Steyning Valley is out to the right. There is a wooden signpost on the left which tells us that Steyning is one and a half miles away, and we carry on following the signs for the Way. Ahead of us is Steyning Bowl. New Hill Barn is just visible through the rain.

There is another post on the left for Steyning as we travel downhill again, now on a tarmac road that sweeps around the outskirts of the Bowl. We stop and ask a man out walking his dog the name of the road, but he doesn't know. We carry on, following the signs for the South Downs Way, which lead us around the edge of the bowl and in better weather is a popular spot for hang gliders. Down in the bowl is Upper Mauding Farm. My phone rings. It's Jim. 'Stay where you are, we'll come and pick you up.' I explain we're on the top of Steyning Bowl, but Jim's none the wiser and says he will ring me back.

We follow the road for about a mile. The trail itself is just to the other side of a wire fence, but with the rain the footpath is a sea of mud, so we stick to the tarmac. At the edge of the Bowl, the Way goes through a wooden gate off to the left. There are open fields both sides here and we can look back and see where we've been walking over an hour ago. Surprisingly, down in the valley there is no mist and visibility is good. We are heading towards Annington Hill. Below, at the far end of the Bowl, is Annington Farm. How I'd love to be sitting in the farmer's cottage down there, beside a blazing log fire, drying out and sipping a nice cup of hot sweet tea! But I ain't. I'm fucking soaking wet and still have about three miles to go.

Martin, who is about 50 yards behind Paul and me, suddenly shouts excitedly, 'Jim's on the phone and he's parked up near the cement works on the Shoreham Road.' I check

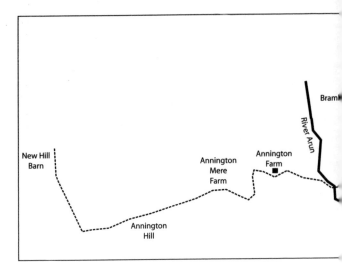

New Hill Barn

Annington Mere Farm

Annington Farm

Bram

River Arun

Annington Hill

my map and tell Martin we are about half a mile away. I shout back, 'Tell him we will meet him in the car park near the bridge which crosses the River Adur.' Martin talks into his phone. Jim says he'll be there. Even though he hasn't got a map, he says he will find us. Martin is suffering. Paul drops back to walk with him. His legs are aching and his feet are wet and sore. He's had enough and is mumbling away to himself, 'Fuck this for a game of soldiers, fucking poxy walk, I must be fucking mad, I need my brains testing.'

'Not far now, Mart,' I shout back over my shoulder, not bothering to look back for an answer or reaction. The pair of them have dropped back and Martin stops for a breather. I can hear Paul coaxing him along. His legs start moving again. The cement works where Jim and Terry were comes into view. It's downhill all the way now. I can see the little church of Botolphs with its stone roof. This Saxon hamlet has a timber-framed clergy house. The rain begins to ease. Why didn't it five hours ago?

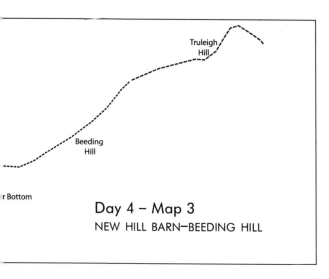

Truleigh
Hill

Beeding
Hill

r Bottom

Day 4 – Map 3
NEW HILL BARN–BEEDING HILL

There's a double track covered by trees for the next 500 yards as the path sweeps off to the left. At the bottom of the lane it's out onto a tarmac road right past Mulberry Cottage. I carry on over the disused railway line which runs over 50 miles from Shoreham to Guildford in Surrey. It's called the Downs Link and, so I'm told, is a lovely long bike ride or walk. Nigel's done it and says it's well worth doing. It also links the South and North Downs. We have passed Annington Farm and now have a good view of the little church on the right-hand side.

There's a bridle bridge up ahead, and standing there waving his arms in the air like he's waiting at the top of Everest for us is Jim. He runs towards us. We all stop and he greets us with a warm handshake. 'Where's Terry?' I ask.

'In the car,' replies Jim. 'He said he ain't getting out of the motor in bleeding weather like this.' Sensible Terry!

We cross the bridge over the fast-flowing River Adur. We have been walking for five and a half hours and covered just over 13 miles. Just before the car park we pass a water tap. The sound of loud music fills the air. Inside the car is Time Warp Tel, singing along to the Small Faces at the top of his voice, his sheepskin coat fastened up to his neck. He winds down the steamed-up window of the car. 'Cold enough, boys?' he asks as we strip off and throw our drenched clothes into the boot of the car. Jim hands me a dry sweatshirt. Always bring waterproof jacket and trousers and dry clothing to change into if you get wet. I take my rucksack off and take out my camera, which is filled with rainwater. Two inches of water is lying in the bottom of my bag. I can't say that I've enjoyed today. I'm soaked to the skin and on the other days I've walked, the views from high on the Downs have been spectacular. Today in some parts you couldn't see 10ft in front of you, but, still, I'm now over halfway along the South Downs Way.

We stop for a pint in the Castle at Bramber, where I stopped the first night on the cycle ride, and sit around the imitation log fire. The usual suspects are in here and the 4 X 4 crowd have filled up the car park. I take off my socks and drape them over the fireguard, then warm my feet on the fake flames. Jim gets a round in and breaks out the celebratory cigars. Some of the locals stare at us in disbelief, and after we've dried out somewhat we head off to my local for a meal and a few more pints. Martin is as pleased as punch he has managed to walk so far, and he did do well. He even hands me a cheque for £250 made out to the Cherries, the children's centre in Chichester I'm raising money for. But I know from experience that tomorrow he'll really begin to feel the aches and pains. Still, it was a good day and this time I've had no problems with my feet. A good pair of boots makes the job so much easier.

TOURIST INFORMATION
Worthing Tel: 01903 210022
Shoreham-By-Sea Tel: 01273 452086

YOUTH HOSTELS
Arundel Tel: 01903 88 2204
(There is also a campsite just off the A24 at Washington.)

TAXIS
4 By 5 Private Hire, Chiltington Tel: 01798 815555
Castle Cars, Arundel Tel: 01903 884444
Lyns Cars, Worthing Tel: 01444 243207
M J Private Hire, Storrington Tel: 01903 745414

BUSES
The number 289 goes from Storrington to Washington
The numbers 1 and 2 serve Horsham and Worthing from the A24 near Washington
The number 100 runs from Washington to Steyning and Bramber

RAILWAY
The nearest on this stretch is Amberley, Pulborough, Arundel, Littlehampton or Worthing

PLACES OF INTEREST
St Mary's House, Bramber
Wiston House, near Steyning
The Model bakery at Steyning, for excellent homemade cakes and snacks
Maharajah Indian restaurant, Bramber

The Walk – Day Five
UPPER BEEDING–A27 CROSSING

AFTER THE RAIN, STORMS, tornadoes and hurricanes in Sussex over the last few months, it's nice to see on the weather forecast that a dry, sunny day is in store for the next day, Tuesday, 15 November. I pack my rucksack, this time including my newly purchased wet-weather gear. There's no way I'm ever going to get caught out again; after the drowning me, Martin and Paul got the last time we were up on the Downs, I'm determined to stay as dry as I can.

I phone Keith and arrange for him to pick me up at 7 a.m. tomorrow.

The next morning he's there on the dot. We have breakfast in a café in Shoreham, and at 9 a.m. he drops me off in the car park on Shoreham Road, the place where Time Warp Tel and Jim the builder picked me and the boys up after the last section of the walk. I bid farewell to Keith and as usual he wishes he were coming with me. He shakes my hand. 'See ya, King,' he shouts as he zooms off.

I walk to the end of the car park and cross the road to where there is a wooden post pointing in the direction of the South Downs Way. The Way goes through the centre of ploughed fields. It is a cold, fresh day with patches of mist. It was raining earlier, but now the sun is trying to break through. I'm heading up towards Beeding Hill along a farm

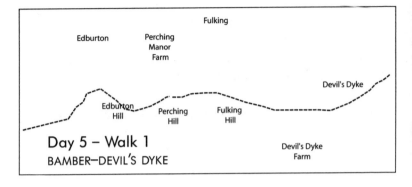

Fulking

Edburton   Perching
                Manor
                Farm

                                                    Devil's Dyke

            Edburton
              Hill   Perching   Fulking
                            Hill   Hill

Day 5 – Walk 1
BAMBER–DEVIL'S DYKE   Devil's Dyke
                                            Farm

track wide enough to take a vehicle. A mist is sitting around the top of the hill. To my right is Anchor Bottom and next to that is the disused cement works with its tall chimney, which can be seen for miles around. South of that I can see Lancing College, with its Gothic spires. The views get even better after about a mile. When I look out to the left I get superb vistas of Bramber and its castle, Steyning, Upper Beeding and Castletown, where there is a mock medieval chateau which is in fact a convent school.

The sun breaks through. I can see the sea out towards Shoreham, with two big tankers out on the horizon. The path is a flint track, which is surprisingly dry, and I climb here quite steadily. Windmill Hill is in the distance and planes taking off or landing at Gatwick pass overhead in the now-clear blue skies. Looking back out towards Steyning Bowl, the mist gives the Downs an almost mountainous feel, although the traffic is still audible down below on the A283. The River Adur, which runs parallel to the road, looks like a lake where it has burst its banks and flooded the surrounding fields. The cars on the road below look like Dinky toys as I climb steadily uphill.

At the top I go through a wooden bridle gate and am rewarded by good views of the English Channel out to the left. The Way cuts through a field here with a deep, dry valley on the right. Here the route goes through another wooden gate and onto a tarmac road, where you will find a car park and a burnt-out car. The Way goes straight on. Follow the tarmac road past a blue plastic council grit box. There are good views to the left and it's clear how badly the downland villages have been affected by the recent storms and high winds. Vast areas of land are under water. The actual South Downs Way is 10ft to the left of the road, but it's a sea of mud, so I'm sticking to the tarmac and keeping my feet dry.

Down below there's a chalk pit with a couple of farms next to it. I'm heading towards Truleigh Hill, and along this bit of road there are good views as far out as the North Downs, and Chanctonbury Ring behind with a vineyard beyond it, towards Lurgshall. Up in front I can see a couple of radio masts and some farm buildings. To the left is a stile, which leads down to Golding Barn. I pass some fir trees on both sides of the path and on the right is a green barn and a cottage, where the occupant's washing, hanging out to dry on a line, sways in the breeze. It's a glorious morning and so far I haven't seen a soul.

The tarmac road now becomes a flint track. I pass under the pine trees and come to a building that looks like a council office or a community centre, or a children's home. In fact it's Tottington Barn youth hostel, a converted 1930s summerhouse. There's a water tap here and if you want bed and breakfast and an evening meal then this is the place. The hostel is well equipped and after a hard day's walk or cycle, I'm sure you won't care what the outside looks like – the last thing on your mind would be the architecture, although I don't suppose Prince Charles will give it any design awards. But it is a strange-looking building to find up on the South Downs. It's like finding a farm halfway down London's

Oxford Street or tractor repairs in Park Lane. There's a notice outside that says, 'This youth hostel welcomes all young people regardless of creed, colour or religion'. But what about people like me, who are getting on and are over 40? Is the Tottington Barn hostel running an ageist regime?

The way widens out here and it's the width of a normal main road. Freshcome Farm is on your right. The two masts I could see about a mile back have another two masts alongside them. There are good views of the sea out to the right. Bed and breakfast is advertised on the gatepost of one of the cottages, just past the farm. In the distance I can see the high-rise buildings that stretch along the coast towards Brighton.

I meet the first person so far today, a man out walking his old Labrador. He says hello and the dog waddles up to me and wags his muddy, wet tail. When I'm about 50 yards past them, out of a field on my left comes a large German Shepherd dog which bounds towards me. I'm frozen to the spot. I don't move a muscle. For a second I have thoughts of being mauled. I don't fucking need this, I'm thinking. What is it with dogs and me? On the first day of the ride I had Lady Penelope's mutts taking a dislike to me, and now this. To my relief the man whistles and the dog veers off in his direction. Phew, that was close. I speed up and check over my shoulder to see where the dog is. I'm OK, he's busy chasing something else now.

I pass the main mast or aerial on my right. On the left below the other three there is a small building that looks like a clubhouse or a football changing-room and I pass a green barn to the right, with what looks like 'Belvedere' painted on the outside wall. There are cows grazing off to the right with good views of the sea out in the distance. On the wire fence around one of the radio masts is the sign NTL, so it must be something to do with a communications company. At the back of the green barn there is a 30ft-high metal feed hopper. I head downhill, towards Edburton Hill. On this part of the Way there are noticeably few trees growing. It's very barren. About half a mile away I notice a man walking three dogs. From here there are good views down onto Shoreham Harbour. The weather is very tranquil, and is hopefully the start of an Indian summer.

When I've been walking for just over an hour I reach a wooden bench where there's a sign telling me that this part of the Downs is the Fulking Escarpment. Down below it is Edburton village, where you will find a shop that specialises in smoked salmon, so pack some bagels and cream cheese and that's your lunch taken care of. For me it's time for a drink and a Mars Bar, so I plonk myself down and look out into the distance towards the weald, where I can hear the sound of shotguns popping. In the village below I can see a church and a barn which has been converted into a house. Then I haul my rucksack back on, climb over a metal farm gate, and tread carefully through the deep mud heading towards Edburton Hill. I pass a couple of grey metal drinking troughs on the way.

The sun is out now, so I take my jacket off and walk in just my sweatshirt and top. As I go, I watch the man I saw earlier go to work with his three dogs, whistling and shouting commands as they get busy rounding up the sheep. I stand and watch for five minutes or so. It's an amazing sight. There must be a couple of hundred sheep in the field. It's great to watch. Just to stand out in the open and watch these dogs work is a real spectacle, but I have to admit that if it was on the telly, I wouldn't be that interested and would probably switch it off though close up it's a real treat and makes the hair on the back of my neck stand up on end.

I get talking to the shepherd. His name is Don Fathers and

I soon realise he's a remarkable man. He is 80 years of age and yet he works 365 days of the year, and he enjoys his job so much that he wouldn't dream of taking a day off. Don is what he calls a 'sheep looker', not a shepherd, the difference being that a shepherd can do everything when it comes to the welfare of sheep, from treating minor ailments to clipping a sheep's coat and nails. Years ago shepherds would spend months on end up here on the Downs with their flocks, a wooden hut their only shelter and sheepdogs their only companions.

Don works in all weathers and uses his three dogs, Tess, Meg and Son, to work the 150 acres in between Perching Hill and Trueleigh Hill Barn.

Don, a retired post office clerk, got his first border collie puppy on his retirement and trained it himself. Using a bush to walk around, he'd give the dog various commands and whistles to tell it which way he wanted it to go around the bush. It takes anything from six months to two years to train a dog to a good standard, and when ready the dog can be used in sheepdog trials. Don is proud of his dogs and has even picked up prizes along the way at various trials.

I stand and watch Don go through his paces and it is truly an amazing sight. The two bitches, Tess and Meg, go about splitting the sheep into two groups. Son lays and watches. Don says Son is sometimes too enthusiastic for his own good, and this along with his slight deafness due to age means that Don likes to use him sparingly.

Sometimes Don has 500 sheep to watch over and often on his round he will find a sheep on its back. Once they go over, he tells me, they have a job to get the right way up, a bit like a tortoise.

Don obviously loves his job but the only drawback, he says, is getting his feet wet every day. 'I've tried every type of footwear from Wellington boots and steel toe-capped army boots to proper walking boots, but keeping my feet dry is a major problem,' he explains. Don walks from his house over near Shoreham every day to work these fields and with no trees in which to shelter, the wind and rain can blow right through you. He's not sure how many miles he and his dogs cover in one day, but it sure don't look like it's doing Don any harm. He's in remarkably good condition, and looks nothing like his age.

One thing that bothers him is people not abiding to the country code. People come up on the Downs for the day to have a picnic, and they litter the countryside with their rubbish, leave gates open and let their dogs chase the sheep. If people would only use their common sense, the countryside would be a better place for everyone. Another thing that worries Don is the lack of new blood being attracted to the job of shepherd, or 'sheep looker'. Young men and women just don't seem to be interested. He knows only one young local man who works his dog.

As we talk, a sheep comes down the path on my side of the wire fence. Don looks to see if it is one of his that has got out, but the colour of the markings on its back tells him that the sheep is from a neighbouring farm.

He carries a mobile phone, the one piece of modern technology he has with him. He laughs as he pulls it from his coat pocket. It was a present from his daughter, who insists he carries it in case of emergency. It's great watching this man and his dogs in action and the talk goes from mobile phones to boxing on television. We chat a while longer and I leave Don to get on with his work. We bid one another farewell, and as I carry on with my journey I can hear the sound of Don's whistles and commands drifting across the valley. A very nice man and a real gent.

After leaving Don, I head up towards Perching Hill. It's very muddy along here, so I'm avoiding the path and walking

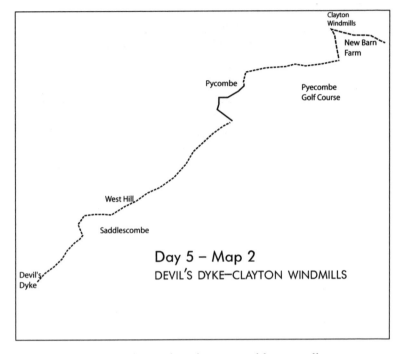

Day 5 – Map 2
DEVIL'S DYKE–CLAYTON WINDMILLS

Clayton
Windmills

New Barn
Farm

Pycombe

Pyecombe
Golf Course

West Hill

Saddlescombe

Devil's
Dyke

on the grass, where the sheep would normally graze. Overhead there are aircraft going in and out of Gatwick and they leave a white plume of smoke behind them in the sky.

I've been walking for an hour and a half. The landscape is very much like the hilly regions of Wales or southern Ireland. The landscape is totally different on this section of the Downs to that of the area around Winchester and down towards Cocking, where there are mile upon mile of woodland. I go over the top of Perching Hill and am now heading up towards Fulking Hill. No, I'm not swearing for a change, that's a real name. Out to the right, just off the Way, are the remains of Fulking isolation hospital, said to have been used during World War One. As I look back behind me, I can see the man and his dogs still hard at work rounding up the sheep.

From the top of the hill I can see the Devil's Dyke Hotel. There are cows grazing in the field and there is a concrete gun bunker, probably dating from around World War Two – there are a few of these scattered along the length of the South Downs. This is a good place to stop for refreshments or a rest and take in the views, though I press on through the field at the bottom of the hotel and go out the wooden gate and across the road, where I pick up the signs for the Way. I can see another radio mast on my right and the clubhouse for the Dyke Golf Club is just obscured by some bushes on the other side of the road. It's quite dry along here and the Way is a chalk and flint track. On the left the Devil's Dyke comes into view. This deep, dry valley was probably formed in the Ice Age and as the ice melted the water cut its way into the chalk. There is a sign here indicating that you are now on Summers Down.

I've been walking for two hours and ten minutes. Across the other side of the Dyke I can see a group of about a dozen walkers dressed in bright red-and-yellow waterproof jackets and the A27 road is visible out towards Brighton. There's a car park in front of me with a burnt-out car, the second one I've seen today. I thought you only saw burnt-out cars in the towns and inner cities, but it just shows you crime is everywhere these days, even up here on the South Downs Way.

I follow the track, which takes me around the edge of the car park and downhill past the iron railing fence of a waterworks. There are a few white cottages and a church out beyond the Dyke in the distance. At a guess I'd say that is the small village of Poynings. At the bottom of the hill I go through a wooden gate and then turn left out onto the road. Once across the other side there's a wooden signpost directing walkers back on to the South Downs Way, and then it's past a house on the right with some sheep in the back garden and through a wooden gate on the left where there's a sign for

New Timber Hill. Here the Way is quite chalky and it leads around the back of Saddlescombe Farm. One of the outbuildings houses a donkey wheel, which many years ago would have been used as a power source for the farm. This interesting piece of local history looks like a giant hamster's wheel. On the right there are a few cream-coloured cottages with green doors. I can hear the sound of dogs barking behind one of the buildings. The last cottage has chickens and geese wandering around, and bundles of hay wrapped in black bags on the left. The smells of the farm fill the air and attack your nostrils – in fact, it fucking stinks.

Then I head through another wooden gate and come out onto a steep, narrow chalk track going up to West Hill. Half-a-dozen horse riders squeeze past me as I step to one side, gingerly manoeuvring their mounts downhill and leaving behind piles of steaming horse shit, which I manage to dodge. There are keen gardeners in London who'd pay good money to have that spread around their prize roses. The rag-and-bone man who used to come round on his horse and cart when I was a kid growing up in south London would sell it for a penny a bucket – and in those days for one penny you could treat your wife or girlfriend to the pictures, have a few drinks in the pub before and fish and chips afterwards, catch a black cab home and still have change in the morning for 20 fags and a paper. At least, that's what my dad used to tell me.

After 100 yards there is another wooden gate, and in the field on the other side are around a dozen horses running loose. They canter over to take a look at me and seem to be defying me to pass. One rolls over and lies looking up at me. I wave my arms in the air and whistle and clap, and they all move off. If they hadn't I don't know what I'd have done.

I look behind me and the views are magnificent. To the right is the sea with the sun shining brightly down on it and

I can see the trees of Chanctonbury Hill and beyond it Bury Hill. In the field is an electric fence that runs its entire length, and a post on the right points out the direction the West Sussex Border Path runs.

I go through another wooden gate at the top of the hill and as I look back I can see three out of the four radio masts back at Truleigh Hill. The horses come back and gather around the gate. One of them gallops towards me, and at the last second puts his brakes on and nearly skids into the barbed-wire fence, only just missing it. This spooks the rest of them and they race off. They look well fed and kept, and probably belong to the local riding school down in Pyecombe.

As I head downhill in the direction of Pyecombe village, out to the right are good views of Brighton and I can see the M23 motorway as it reaches the outskirts of Brighton, and the bridge that crosses it. In front of me on a far hill are two windmills. A petrol station and a church stand out among the rooftops of the village. At the bottom of the hill is a metal farm gate where there is a farmer whose name, it turns out, is Roy, working away cutting a hedge with his JCB machine. He holds the gate open for me as I pass through. We stop and chat and I learn a lot about his job.

Working from 7 a.m. to 7 p.m. seven days a week isn't everyone's ideal job. Throw in 450 ewes, 14 rams and 530 acres of corn, rape, peas, spring barley and wheat to sow and harvest and you'll have some idea of just how hard farmer Roy Goldsmith of Pangdean Farm works.

Roy's parents were farmers and Roy was born into the farming life. But times have changed so much that in the last ten years Roy has had to move away from traditional farming and into more profitable areas. The farm used to employ 23 full-time and many part-time staff, but since restrictions were placed on British farmers by ridiculous EU policies Roy is one farmer who has put other ideas into practice. Along with two gamekeepers he runs a very successful 80-acre shoot. There are 9,000 pheasants and 15,000 partridges. Cover crop has been planted for the birds and every angle of safety is covered; the gamekeepers and beaters carry walkie-talkies and everything is double-checked before a shot can be fired. It ain't cheap to have a day's shooting at Pangdean Farm. It costs £1,000 a gun and only nine guns a day are allowed. Companies pay for clients to enjoy a day's shooting; the corporate entertainment crowd has now moved from Wimbledon and Ascot to the wilds of Sussex, but I can't see Sir Cliff Richard singing 'Summer Holiday' if rain stops play!

Another of Roy's business ventures is the social events he organises in his barns. He does doing a roaring trade – many people want a rustic feel to their wedding receptions, birthday parties, anniversaries or bar mitzvahs.

In the summer, if the weather is good, Roy can sometimes find himself working 15 hours a day. He enjoys working the three dogs he has on the farm: a working border collie for the sheep, a Jack Russell for ratting and a pet Labrador. This year with all the torrential rain and floods in the south, Roy says that some farmers have lost thousands of pounds in ruined seeds and crops. What with dairy farming all but finished, other farmers will have no option but to follow Roy and look to alternative methods of making a living.

Our chat has been really interesting but I eventually have to drag myself away and continue my journey.

From here the Way turns left, out onto a tarmac road. There's smoke coming from behind a hedge, my first bonfire of the day. The Plough Inn is facing me but I'm separated from a nice cold pint of Guinness by six lanes of thundering traffic. The M23 runs right outside the pub, but it is still a haven for the thirsty and hungry and a very good place to call in and have a few drinks or something to eat. Walkers and cyclists are made more than welcome, even those with muddy footwear. I go past the front entrance to Brendon's riding school and turn left over the bridge. The noise of the traffic is almost deafening. There's a road sign here that tells me Brighton is six miles and Crawley is sixteen miles. The Patcham Youth Hostel is two miles away on the A23, just south of the A27 at Patcham Place. Buses run from here into the centre of Brighton. I carry on towards Church Hill, with Pyecombe Church on the right, a small, Norman flint church with a tiled roof and a weather vane on the top, and inside, although a bit on the small side, it houses an unusual lead font.

I've been walking three and a half hours now, only stopping to watch Don, the shepherd, and Roy, the farmer. I follow the tarmac road past a white bungalow-type house called The Chapel, and beyond the village noticeboard at the bottom of School Lane is the A273 road. A signpost tells you Clayton is one mile, Burgess Hill five miles, Haywoods Heath eight, Patcham three, Brighton six, Hassocks two and Ditchling three miles. I turn left here.

The South Downs Way runs parallel to the main road, with a small waterworks on the right and open downs to the left. The path I'm on has a small hedge running alongside it. At the end of the hedge there are signs on the left and right for Pyecombe Golf Club. Cross here – the South Downs Way runs through the car park past the clubhouse on the right and cuts straight through the middle of the golf course, so there are people playing on either side as I walk. As the track for the Way slowly rises, I notice a lawnmower company called Mower Master on the left. I look behind towards New Timber Hill and the route I've been walking for the last hour. The sun is out and it's a glorious day.

The track turns quite muddy at the top of the golf course,

where the Way goes left towards New Barn Farm. Ahead there are good views of the two windmills, which are now less than a mile away. I pass New Barn Farm with its numerous outbuildings and horses grazing, the sunlight giving a silken shine to their coats. At the top of the track the Way goes right. The windmills can be reached down a lane to the left. When I did the cycle ride with the boys we somehow managed to miss the windmills. Whether we sped by too fast and missed them or took a wrong turn I don't know, but today, with the sun out, I must take a look. The larger one of the two is called Jack and is privately owned. Jill, the small white mill, is open on Sundays but only during the summer months.

I stop for a drink and sit on the fence with good views of Burgess Hill and Haywoods Heath. It's well worth a visit up here. If you've got kids, they'd love it. By road the Clayton windmills are reached by Mill Lane off Clayton Lane, just north of Pyecombe. I head back and pick up the South Downs Way. I take off my sweatshirt and walk in only a T-shirt. Although it's the middle of November the sun is very strong. No need for any wet-weather gear today!

I've been walking now for four hours, going uphill on a pebble track. Two people up ahead are walking their Labrador dogs, which are both covered in mud – they look as though they've been having fun. A man passes me walking his Weimaraner dog, which makes a change from a Lab; the Labrador seems to be a prized fashion accessory up here. I've never seen so many people up on the Downs in one day. After weeks of high winds and rain, people are rushing out to catch the rays of the sun for a change.

As I walk, to my left I can see right out towards Kent. I pass a dried-up dew pond and on the right, further along, is the wooden Keymer Post, which points towards Winchester, Eastbourne, Keymer and Brighton. Letters carved on it tell me that Peter and Phillipa loved each other September 1994, blah, blah, blah. The last bit I can't quite make out.

Here I cross from West Sussex into East Sussex, and I don't feel a thing. I carry on through a field full of cows, some armed with huge horns, but if one is brave enough to come near me they will get my size tens up their arse. It's very muddy but level here.

Another dew pond comes up on the left. This one has a wire fence around it with a stile, so that if you want you can get closer and take a better look. It's just sheep and cattle grazing everywhere and there are no trees. It's a very barren landscape. It's beginning to cloud over and so I put my sweatshirt back on. On the right is another dew pond, which cattle are drinking from. One is having a shit at the same time. Christ, that must flavour it no end; I bet it tastes nice to the others!

I reach the top of the hill that runs down into Ditchling Beacon car park. The wind gets up and so it's on with the jacket. When I cycled up here in July it was shorts and T-shirt weather, but today the sun has gone in and the chill reminds me it's November. I make my way into the car park. The annual London to Brighton Bike Ride goes past here and there are not many people who manage to cycle up this steep hill. If they do, or they say they have, they are either fit or telling porkies. Normally in the car park there's a van where you can buy ice creams, lollies and drinks, but today, since I've run out of liquid refreshment, it isn't here – typical of my luck. As usual the car park is busy, with nearly every space taken. People come up here to sit, chat and take in the views, which are fabulous. I cross the road towards a dew pond which faces me.

Here the route goes between two 2ft-high rocks and through a wooden gate. Follow the signs for the South Downs Way. There is an information board telling you how

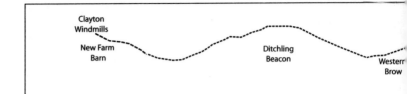

Clayton
Windmills

New Farm
Barn

Ditchling
Beacon

Western
Brow

Day 5 – Map 3
CLAYTON WINDMILLS—HOUSEDOWN FARM

dew ponds are formed. It says that clay is laid on top of chalk
and the ponds are filled by dew, mist and rainfall. The track
here is very muddy and open and there are no trees, just mile
upon mile of open, rolling downs with good views on both
sides. I'm going in the direction of Western Brow and Streat
Hill. Plumpton Agricultural College, the racecourse and
Plumpton Place can be seen at the foot of the Downs. A V-
shaped woodland planted to commemorate Queen Victoria's
golden jubilee in 1887 can still be seen on this stretch of the
Downs. Streat Hill Farm is off to the right; just below Streat
Hill there is a wooden gate, which leads out onto a tarmac

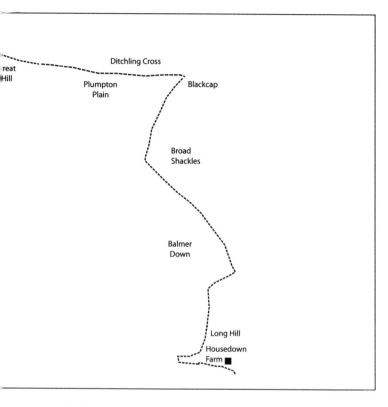

Ditchling Cross

reat
Hill

Plumpton
Plain

Blackcap

Broad
Shackles

Balmer
Down

Long Hill

Housedown
Farm

road called Streat Bostall. If you turn right onto this road it runs down towards the University of Sussex at Falmer.

The track for the Way carries straight on here, towards Plumpton Plain. It's an ideal track for biking, with the Way both flat and dry. Next I come to Plumpton Bostall, where a stony track that veers off to the left runs down to the Half-moon pub where there's a caravan and campsite near the college. On the right is an old wooden fence post with a path that leads down to a Bronze Age settlement. The hills and downs off to the right are all different shades of yellow, brown and green. At the end of Plumpton Plain is a wooden gate that leads through to Blackcap. On the left are the Beeches, a small wood. The South Downs Way runs down to the right on a single muddy track, where even if you stick to the sides of the path your feet will sink ankle-deep into the mud. My boots and socks, which I've tucked my tracksuit bottoms into, soon get a plastering of mud.

It begins to spit with rain and as a black cloud looms overhead the spit soon turns to heavy rain and the heavens open up. It's on with the waterproof trousers, but that's easier said than done as the mud on my boots makes it nearly impossible to pull the trousers on. Up here there is no shelter. I get the trousers on eventually, with a struggle, but there's no way I'm ever going to get caught out again by the weather, not after the last soaking I got with Paul and Martin. I carry on for about a mile. Ashcombe Bottom is out to the left and in the distance I can see the converted grandstand of the old Lewes racecourse. It's downhill through the mud with the path flanked on both sides by thorn hedges. There is no way you could cycle along here – the deep mud makes it too dangerous and only the daft and Keith would attempt it.

I've been walking for five and a half hours and I've got no blisters for a change; my investment in a good pair of walking boots seems to have paid off. It's only the second time I've worn them but they feel like a good pair of indoor slippers.

I pass an old post set in the middle of a path. Just past here the Way turns left and goes under some electricity lines. Off to the left three farmers in their tractors are ploughing their fields. I'm heading downhill, on a double farm track for another mile, past peacefully grazing sheep. A crow bathes itself in a dew pond. I can hear the sound of the traffic on the A27 Lewes to Brighton road so I can't be far from civilisation. There's a patch of woodland off to the right and the Way splits at the bottom near a stile. The new route takes you via Housedown Farm and opened in 1997. The old route is the one we took when we cycled the Way and it has now been downgraded to a public footpath. In the summer it was a 6ft-high cornfield, and now it's been ploughed. I don't have very fond memories of my previous journey here and laugh to myself as I turn right and head off, following the signs for the Way. I go through the gate and head downhill, with a barbed-wired fence either side. At the bottom of the valley is an electricity sub-station. Turn left here and follow the uphill zig-zag path through the woods. It's dry but the fallen leaves make it slippery underfoot. I stop and catch my breath; the hill is steep and after walking for over six hours my legs are aching. At the top of the woods on Long Hill there is a wooden gate and where the woods join a ploughed field there is a telecommunications mast, which sadly spoils the view out towards Lewes.

Next I head downhill towards Housedown Farm and in the distance I can see two masts on a hill, which I think is towards Beddingham Hill, where the Way runs out to Alfriston. I can see the white chalk hills on the outskirts of Lewes. There is a rainbow in the sky but a black cloud moves in. With all the rain the people of East Sussex have had in the last three months, the last thing anybody needs is more of it. I wouldn't wish what the people of Lewes and the surrounding areas have recently gone through on my worst enemy.

As I reach the bottom of the hill there is a flint wall surrounding Housedown Farm. I go down half-a-dozen stone steps and out through a gate onto a tarmac sliproad, which runs alongside the A27. This is where the Way ends for me today, though it continues on the other side of the A27, which you can reach via a nearby footbridge. If you turn right here, about half a mile along is a petrol station, where you can buy refreshments. I'm heading up towards Falmer now, which is about a mile and a half away. I've been walking for six and a half hours and I'm going to jump on a bus outside Sussex University and head into Brighton for a nice curry and a few bottles of Indian lager. I think I deserve it.

TOURIST INFORMATION
Shoreham Tel: 01273 452086
Hove Tel: 01273 778087

YOUTH HOSTELS
Truleigh Hill Tel: 01903 882204
Patcham Tel: 01273 556196

TAXIS
Access Taxis, Shoreham Tel: 01273 203200
Brighton and Hove Radio Cabs Tel: 01273 204060

BUSES
The number 20 bus runs from Bramber town centre to Shoreham, Hove and Brighton

RAILWAY
The nearest railway stations are at Shoreham, Hove, Brighton or Falmer

PLACES OF INTEREST
Historic Brighton
Shoreham airport
Brighton Marina

The Walk – Day Six
A27 CROSSING–ALFRISTON

IT'S TUESDAY, 5 DECEMBER, a grey, cloudy winter's day. Rain has been forecast to reach this part of East Sussex by midday. I was bright and early and by 8 a.m. I'm setting off. I've had breakfast over in Shoreham and my aim is to finish this part of the walk before the wet weather sets in.

I park the car in a lay-by right next to the A27 and pick up where I left off on the last walk, outside Housedown Farm. From here I walk to a bridge that spans both sides of the A27; I'm not going to risk my life trying to cross four lanes of fast-moving traffic. At the other side of the bridge is a tarmac road. This runs down to a gate that leads onto a path running parallel to a railway line. I follow the muddy single track until I see a sub-station in front of me, then turn right and go under a brick archway, which runs under the railway line.

The Way turns left onto a chalk path, then right after 50 yards and heads uphill. After 200 yards the Way sweeps left. New Barn is out on the right. Go through a clump of trees, up a slight hill and through a wooden bridle gate, which I have trouble opening and closing; it looks like the spring lock is knackered. The valley of Cold Coombes is on the left. Sheep graze peacefully as the cold wind whistles. The lights of Lewes town twinkle in the dawn light out in the distance. It's

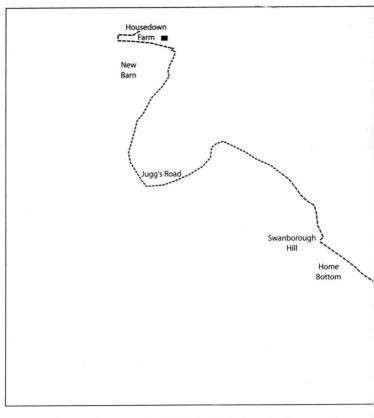

overcast, but with a bit of luck I'll finish before the forecasted downpour.

It's uphill for over a mile with the woods of Newmarket Plantation on the right and open countryside to the left. The landscape here is very bleak. When I come to a farm gate it all becomes a bit confusing. The signs with the acorn on are here, but they don't really explain which path to take so I choose the one that runs around the edge of Cold Coombes. I stop and look back to where I have just come from. The lights of Lewes are still on and traffic is visible on the A27

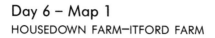

Day 6 – Map 1
HOUSEDOWN FARM–ITFORD FARM

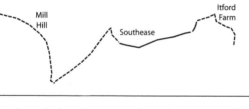

Mill Hill

Southease

Itford Farm

down below. I can see the radio mast at the top of Long Hill, and above that the clump of trees above Blackcap. Most of the fields have been ploughed ready for next year's crops. The wind whistles around my head as I pull the collar of my coat up.

I'm still heading uphill. Looking back I can see the Sussex University site at Falmer. This part of the trail is called Juggs Road, and was once an ancient route used for carrying fish from the coast to Lewes Market. The fish were kept fresh throughout the journey in pottery jugs, hence the name.

Behind you, you can see out towards the radio masts at Truleigh Hill. I can remember cycling down Truleigh Hill I'm on, which goes from Swanborough Hill right down to the A27. On that day in July Keith, as usual, was going so fast he had trouble stopping and nearly went over the gate at New Barn. There are two radio masts on the right, but the path I'm on goes uphill towards two dew ponds with gorse bushes surrounding them. Here the path is very muddy. I've been walking for just over an hour.

In the distance up in front are another couple of radio aerials, but they are probably five or six miles away up at Beddingham Hill. I go past the dew ponds, and again the route gets confusing. Out come the maps and after a while I choose the path that leads to my right. I'm on the right path, as I reach another dew pond with a stile that is marked on the map. The pond has a fence around it, and on one of the posts is the sign pointing out the direction for the South Downs Way. I'm on the right track. I have clear views now back out towards Bramber, which is a six-hour walk from where I started today. From here I have good views of Lewes and the surrounding hills. Below that are the small towns of Kingston and Itford. A train with three carriages runs along the line between Lewes and Falmer. It is so peaceful up here. The only sounds are the wind and the odd bird singing.

I'm now heading towards Swanborough Hill, where the Way goes right. After passing through a gate, after 50 yards I turn left down a concrete path wide enough to take a vehicle. I see my first people of the day; two farmers pass me driving their pick-up trucks, with what looks to be homing pigeons in wicker baskets on the back. It's downhill for about three miles, and at one point near White Way I cross the Greenwich Meridian and pass from the eastern hemisphere into the western. Good views can be had of Lewes, which seems to be getting nearer as I come around in a large semi-circle. County Hall seems to grab most of the landscape, but the Norman castle and various Georgian buildings can also be picked out. I pass three stones, each around a foot high. They all have holes with a circumference of about three-quarters of an inch in them. It looks like a tethering point. A sea of mud surrounds the stones, and there must be a couple of hundred sheep just in this one field. I would hazard a guess that the stones are something to do with them.

I'm heading up towards Mill Hill. Beady Bottom Farm is about a mile and a half out to the right. I cross more ploughed fields, go through a gate and then down an alley of bushes. At the end of it, on the right is a large *Dallas*-style house complete with a Range Rover parked outside. There is another property on the left, but the South Downs Way carries on through a gate and crosses a field of cows towards Beady Bottom Farm, which is down below in a valley. The *Dallas*-style house, called Mill Hill House, is on a tarmac road which runs from here down into Rodmell village, which is also the alternative route avoiding the main road between Southease and Rodmell. This less hazardous route via Rodmell takes in Monks House, where Leonard and Virginia Woolf once lived, and which is now owned by the National Trust. I take the traditional route because being a London boy, I'm used to dealing with traffic; it's the cows that frighten me, and the field I'm in has about 20 of the bastards looking at me. Some are armed with horns and as I walk towards them, they ain't in no hurry to get out of the way. I clap my hands together and whistle loudly. 'Go on. Fuck off!' I shout. One moves and then they all move. They stop and look back at me. I feel better now. 'Don't fuck with me,' I shout at them. Clint Eastwood, eat your heart out. A couple of hundred yards further on, they get their own back when I tread in cow shit and my boots sink up to the ankles in the stuff.

I go through the gate at the bottom of the field and past the outskirts of the farm, which looks like Steptoe's yard. There are bits of rusty, rotting machinery, and it don't smell too good either. I turn right onto a tarmac road and leave the farm behind me. After about three-quarters of a mile, the Way goes through a wooden gate, uphill across a field and then out through yet another gate onto a tarmac road. Take the immediate right turn for the Telescombe Youth Hostel, or turn right onto the main road and then first left to pick up the South Downs Way. There is a sign here saying 'Southease Village – No Through Road'.

At the top of the road there is what looks like a brick gun-turret, left over from World War Two. I go downhill past two garages with the doors painted in the garish yellow colour favoured by the Cowdray Estate over near Cocking. There is a post box on the right next to the church, which was built in Saxon times and has an unusual round tower. On the left is Rectory Cottage, which is made of wood. The small churchyard is surrounded by a flint stonewall. Out in front is a small village green, which is a peaceful place to stop for a rest. At the end of the village there is a farm on the left. The River Ouse has overflowed here and the surrounding fields are underwater. I cross the green metal bridge that spans the river, and as I cross I can see in between the heavy wooden slabs the fast-flowing river below me. The alternative route via Rodmell rejoins the Way here. There is a sign on the left that tells you Lewes is four miles along a public footpath.

I leave the bridge and head towards Southease railway station, which is tiny and has no ticket office or staff, although the station is a link between the coast and London and is surprisingly busy, with trains running frequently along this stretch of line. I've been walking now for two hours and

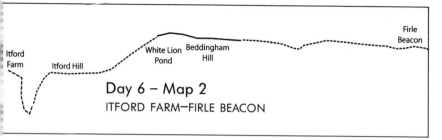

Day 6 – Map 2
ITFORD FARM–FIRLE BEACON

covered around six and a half miles. There is a level crossing
for cars at the station, which drivers have to operate
themselves. Pedestrians cross via a concrete bridge that spans
the tracks. Once through the white gate at the bottom you are
out onto a tarmac road which leads past Itford Farm, which
has a huge barn on the right and a cottage on the left. Here
you will find a tap with fresh drinking water. Fill your bottles
up here, there's nowhere else you can get a drink between here
and Alfriston.

I now have the busy A26 road facing me so I take a right
turn and follow the edge of the road for about 75 yards. I
then pick up the South Downs Way opposite. Be careful
when you cross as the traffic thunders along here, so be very
alert. Once across, the Way goes through a wooden gate and
uphill until you come to yet another set of gates, it now goes
into a steep climb uphill with good views back towards
Southease village. A sign in the ground reads 'Do not cause
erosion – keep to the path'.

I'm heading towards Itford Hill. There are good views on
the right of Newhaven and its port. I walk another one and a
half miles before I reach Itford Hill. From the top of the ridge
there are good views of Lewes and the huge Asham pit. I can
see the lorries loading and unloading from up here and they
look the size of Tonka toys. Up ahead I can see the masts of
Beddingham Hill. I pass Red Lion Pond, which is now dry.

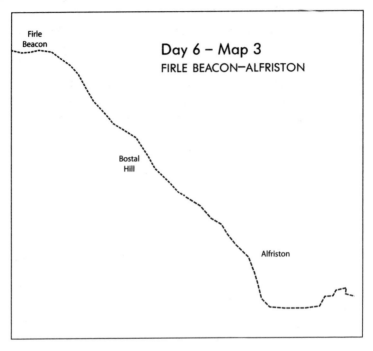

Firle
Beacon

Bostal
Hill

Alfriston

On the right is a sheep-holding pen and just before the masts on the left is White Lion Pond. There are cows everywhere and once again they don't move, but dare me to walk through them. I take my rucksack off and swing it around my head like a lassoo. They soon move and I carry on. I don't trust the bastards. I've seen the TV programme *Vets in Practice* where the vet puts on rubber gloves and sticks his hand right up the cow's arse; well, if they don't get out of the way it'll be my toe going up their arses!

I stop at the radio masts on Beddingham Hill. A wire fence surrounds them and there's a small brick building inside the compound. I've got good views out towards South Heighton and Piddinghoe Pond, which the locals pronounce as 'Pidd'n'oo' and is very popular with windsurfers in the summer. Black Cap Farm is out to the right about two miles down below.

It's very bleak up here. I'm heading towards the car park at Firle Bostal. The wind is blowing a gale and with no trees or cover, there is nowhere to shelter. It is a very desolate part of the Way. I've been walking now for three hours, and have seen no one on foot today, just cows and sheep. I pass through the car park and head up towards Firle Beacon, which is 712ft above sea level. On its ridge there are over 50 Bronze Age barrows. Arlington reservoir is in the distance to the right. This large expanse of water seems to follow you all along this stretch.

The landscape is very grey and dull. Most trees around the Firle area were lost during the great storm and hurricane of 1987; of the 15 to 20 million trees lost in Great Britain that year, about 3 million were destroyed in East Sussex alone. It is clouding over but there is still no sign of the forecast rain. Firle Tower is in the distance on the other side, down on the weald. This was built in 1819 by the fourth Viscount Gage to house his game-keeper; there's a similar structure at Laughton. The story goes that on Lord Gage's return by train from London his servant would wave his handkerchief from the arriving train to alert staff of their master's return. A flag would then be hoisted on either of the two towers and a coachman would be dispatched to pick up his Lordship from Glynde railway station.

I see my first people of the day – two men walking their dogs, a Great Dane and a Jack Russell. The Downs are very muddy here and my feet sink into the sodden grass. Charleston and Tilton Farm are out below. Tilton Woods and Selmeston village disappear out of view as I head first uphill and then down towards the car park at Bopeep Bostal. The path around the edge of the car park is a sea of mud. I take the slightly firmer ground. It's back uphill here and through a set of gates. I've never seen so many gates in one day. This section is full of the poxy things.

At Bostal Hill I stop to check my map. A trail goes off to the right. It's confusing here, but after looking at my map yet again, I take the left fork. A man comes striding up from behind me at a fair old pace and wishes me a good day as he slows down.

'Going far?' he asks.

I tell him I've walked from the A27 crossing and that I'm finishing in Alfriston. He says he's out on his daily constitutional, a five-mile round walk from Alfriston to Bostal Hill. He does it very quickly, almost at power-walking pace. He tells me that he does this walk six times a week and it keeps him trim and fit.

'Don't tell me you're 84 but you think you don't look it and you used to be a paratrooper, and could have been a pro footballer but for war breaking out, and you saved the likes of me?'

He shoots me a blank look and marches off into the distance, his arms and legs pumping away like piston rods.

Alfriston and Berwick are out to the left. I pass a signpost pointing to Berwick. On the right are bundles of soaking and rotting rolled-up hay; grass is now growing on top of them. I get my first sight of Alfriston from here. The Cuckmere River, which runs through the town, looks like it has burst its banks. The route is downhill now all the way. The trail is an uneven chalk surface and very slippery. At the bottom I come out into Kings Ride, which is a street with houses on both sides of the road. I go past the Star Inn and the Forte Heritage hotel.

This is the end of my walk today. I have really marched on and have covered 14 miles. It has taken me just over four and a half hours and the rain has held off. From here I catch a bus to Lewes bus station and then another to where I've parked the car. Both bus drivers are very helpful and the last one even stops where I parked my car. That's service for you.

TOURIST INFORMATION
Lewes Tel: 01273 483448
Seaford Tel: 01323 897426

YOUTH HOSTELS
Telescombe near Rodmell Tel: 01273 301357
Alfriston Tel: 01323 870423

HOTELS
The White Lodge Hotel, Alfriston
Wingrove Inn, Alfriston
Deans Palace Hotel, Alfriston

TAXIS
Lewes and District Taxis Tel: 01273 483232
Long Distance Cars Tel: 01273 486648

BUSES
There's a bus station in Lewes
From Alfriston you can catch the number 125 to Lewes or the 126 to Eastbourne
From Southease the number 123 goes to Newhaven
From Lewes the 20 or 28 will take you to Brighton

RAIL
Lewes, Glynde, Berwick, Polgate, Southease, Newhaven and Seaford all have stations.

PLACES OF INTEREST

The Long Man, Wilmington Hill (a chalk figure cut into the hillside)

Charleston Farmhouse, Firle (discovered by Virginia and Leonard Woolf)

Monks House, Rodmell (the home of the above from 1919)

Drusillas Park and Zoo, Alfriston

Firle Place

Newhaven Fort (built in the 1860s to deter invaders)

The Walk – Day Seven

ALFRISTON–EASTBOURNE

IT'S A GREY, WINDY, overcast morning and the time is 11 o'clock. I'm about to leave the car park at Alfriston for the final leg of the walk between Winchester and Eastbourne. Today's walk is around ten and a half miles, and I estimate that it should take me around three to four hours.

I leave the car park on the edge of the village and go past the tourist information board, which includes details of where to stay, walking and cycle routes and dates of events; there's everything you need to know about the area. Heading up through Alfriston village, I pass the main square and the few tea shops, pubs and gift shops, many of which are half-timbered and date back to the 14th and 15th centuries. Alfriston is one of my favourite villages I've passed through on the Way. It's like taking a step back in time, and whatever the weather, the place has a picturesque feel to it. There is no train station and only a couple of buses a day, so you tend to feel cut off from the hustle and bustle of town or city life.

I pick up the South Downs Way footpath on the other side of the white bridge that stretches over the River Cuckmere. Nearby is a thatched clergy house, which was the first property purchased by the National Trust, in 1896 for £10. The bridleway section via Jevington to Eastbourne is picked up near Plonk Barn, which is about 200 yards ahead of me. I

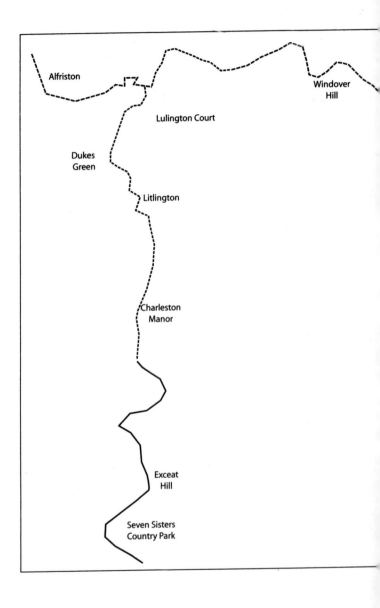

Day 7 – Map 1
ALFRISTON–SEVEN SISTERS

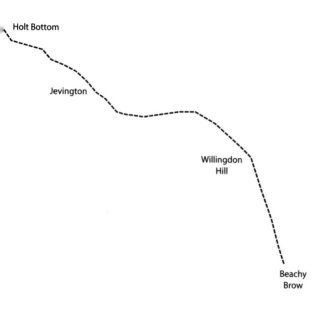

Holt Bottom

Jevington

Willingdon
Hill

Beachy
Brow

make my way down a couple of steps and turn right along the riverbank. The rear of the parish church faces the other side of the fast-flowing brown water of the Cuckmere. The church, which was built in 1360 on the remains of the old St Andrews monastery, is rightly known as the 'Cathedral of the South Downs'. Out to my left I can see where the river levels have risen in the last few months and flooded the surrounding grassy marshes. A couple of swans swim in the water, ducking their heads into the river looking for food, and seagulls fly overhead swirling around in the wind. It is very muddy underfoot.

The village of Litlington comes into view out to the left, which is bounded by woods on one side and on the other by wide water meadows. Folles Manor and Frog Firle Youth Hostel are off to the right. After going through a series of bridle gates I pass a couple of drainage ditches with metal operating wheels that work the metal flaps which when closed stop tidal saltwater flooding onto the nearby marshes. The sound of a hammer banging on brickwork and the rustle of dry reeds fills the air.

I turn left down a narrow tarmac path, which leads into Litlington. I pass the man with the noisy hammer. He looks like he's doing some plumbing, as he pushes a piece of copper pipe through a hole in some brickwork. At the top of the path on a post there's a sign for the South Downs Way. I turn right and go past the Plough and Harrow pub, which I'll remember for a future visit. Across the road are some tea-rooms. At the other end of the village is the small weather-boarded bell tower of St Michaels. A structure was first recorded on this site in 1150 but the building as seen today dates from around 1863.

I am now walking along a tarmac road. I stop outside a thatched cottage and watch a man up a ladder repairing part of the roof. When he comes down to his van to get some tools and water reeds, which he uses for the repairs, we chat about his job and he says there's not enough work to go around among the local thatchers, so travelling hundreds of miles, even abroad, is all part of the job. It's a skilled job, as there's a five-year apprenticeship before you qualify as a thatcher, but with some roofs lasting 60 to 70 years thatchers are hardly likely to go back to the same job twice.

I set off again and after 50 yards take the track to the left. There's a sign here for Clapham Farm and Clapham House, which is steeped in history and controversy; it is said that Maria Fitzherbert, the illicit bride of King George IV, lived a secret life here with her lover and they posed as the Payne family. There is also a sign for Jevington and West Dean on a wooden post, but you could easily miss it (I did) as it's tight up against a flint wall. Almost immediately opposite is another signpost for the Way, a yellow sign with the usual black acorn, and below that there's a stone sign on the ground. This sends me uphill through a bridle gate and out onto a field with grazing horses. You have to be very careful with the signs around Litlington as they tend to be hidden away.

I carry on upwards for about half a mile. Behind me there are good views of the flint cottages and houses of Litlington. Out in the distance, on the other side of Alfriston, are Firle Beacon and Bostal Hill. At the top of the field is a double stile, with just a 10ft gap. Beware – in between the two is ankle-deep mud, made worse by cows crossing from one field to the other. Clapham Barn is on the left and here the Way becomes a single-track path with a gorse hedge running alongside you. Below are good views of the Cuckmere, also known as 'Snake River', as it winds its way down to the sea. As I start to head downhill I catch my first glimpse of

Charleston Manor through the trees that surround it at the bottom of the hill. Sheep graze out to the left just below the trees on the edges of Friston Forest.

Once over a stile I see that the Way is signposted left, and then turns right up the side of Charleston Manor and up some steps cut into the hillside. At the top there is a choice of trails. The South Downs Way is straight ahead. This is Forestry Commission land and I can see where new trees have recently been planted, and tied to a wooden support with white plastic tape. The overhead telephone lines, fir trees and steep rolling hills give this section of the walk an almost alpine feel; apart from the lack of snow, overhead cable cars and skiers, you could be anywhere in the Alps.

I've been walking an hour and a quarter now, and I see the first person of the day, a man out walking his dogs. Heading downhill, the trail goes around to the right. After passing through a gate and coming out onto a road, I arrive in the village of West Dean. If you think Alfriston and Litlington are quaint old English villages then wait till you see West Dean. It really is a picture. Take time out to look around. There's not much to see besides the church, the phone, post box and small pond, but it is a beautiful village with its flint cottages and lack of traffic; unless you live here, there are no parking spaces. It's like going back 100 years in time. I decide to take a look around the parish church of All Saints, which is said to date from Saxon times though its half-hipped spire and oblong bell tower are of a later date. The parsonage next door claims to be one of the oldest inhabited rectories in England.

The man with the dogs I saw earlier is standing outside the church talking to the vicar. We chat and I learn that his dogs are a rare breed called Dogue de Bordeaux, which originally hails from a southern France breed and happens to be one of my favourite breeds of dog. These fawn-coloured mastiff-type dogs were once on the list of dogs banned under the Dangerous Dogs Act, but by nature they are of a calm disposition and although they make an excellent watchdog, they are nonetheless good with children and the appearance of one with Tom Hanks in the film *Turner and Hooch* saw their popularity rise in this country.

I pick up the trail past the green phone box and information board, which is next to the pond. It's uphill again as I climb over 200 steps cut into the hill through an archway of overhanging trees. I guarantee you'll be out of breath before you're halfway up. It's a tough old climb. A group of about 30 elderly walkers pass me going in the opposite direction. Near the top there is a section of flint wall missing. Here one of the many trails in these woods goes off to the right. In front of me is a flint wall. I turn right here and find an information board describing the local geology. A stile cut into the wall houses two wooden seats. There are good views out towards the Seven Sisters park.

I go downhill towards the park's visitor and information centre, which is beside the A259 road. Here there are the Cuckmere Cycle Company (where you can hire bikes), a restaurant, toilets and a drinking tap. Opposite the visitor centre is a bus stop. Cross with care, because there is a blind bend and you can't see the traffic coming from the right. Once across I go through the gate next to the car park and follow the signs for the Way. A route accessible by wheelchair also runs through the park. I head uphill through fields of grazing sheep. There is a marker stone near the top of Exceat Hill indicating the site of a church, which was once part of the now lost village of Exceat. Down below are the remains of pill boxes, those small forts of concrete used as part of Britain's coastal defences during World War Two. The wind really sends a chill through my body and the treeless landscape offers no shelter.

The Way is indicated by low markers and once through the gate at the top, the direction to take can become confusing. I end up down at Foxhole cottages, where there is a camping barn, and walk around the pond outside them for half an hour looking for a sign for the Way before eventually giving up and going back to the wooden gate at the top of the hill, where I retrace my steps. One of the low markers pointing out the direction of the Way has been damaged so I study the map and head back downhill in a westerly direction. At the bottom I find a concrete track and beside it a signpost. I follow the signs for the Way, which take me along a shingle path then through a gate, up some steps and out into open fields. From here it's uphill all the way. There are lots of rabbit burrows dug into the hillside.

I've been walking two hours now, and the higher I go the windier it gets. It must be blowing a force eight or nine. Out to the right are good views of the Cuckmere where it reaches the sea at Cuckmere Haven. The shingle beach is battered by the rolling waves. The wind is easterly, and hits me head-on. I have a wet-weather jacket and trousers on, and the wind gets up my sleeves and trouser legs and puffs me up like the Michelin Man. I'm having trouble moving forward.

It's a long hard climb before I reach Cliff End. Against the wire fence at the top is a dead sheep that looks as though something has taken a bite out of its hind legs and neck. The other sheep don't seem too bothered and carry on grazing around it. The cottages across at Short Cliff, on the other side of the estuary, cling precariously to the hillside and don't look as if they have long to go before they drop into the sea below them. I follow the coastal path, at a height of 400ft above sea

level, along an electric sheep fence which is the only thing
between me and certain death.

From here I start walking the ups and downs of a group of
hills called the Seven Sisters, and boy are they hard. They're
bitches. There are in fact eight of them. Going from the
country park to the Birling Gap, the order they run in is
Haven Brow, Short Brow, Rough Brow, Brass Point, Flagstaff
Point, Flat Hill, Bailys Hill and Went Hill. I've never done
anything like it and the wind is bringing me almost to a
standstill. I'm very conscious of the drop just yards to my
right. The last thing I want is to be lifted up by the winds and
dumped over the edge. How many sheep and dogs have gone
this way?

Trudging up and down these hills is getting on my fucking
nerves. This is definitely the hardest part of the Way I've
walked so far. I stop for a breather and check the map. Out
on the right I can see Crowlink, a part of the National Trust,
and the largest of the National Trust properties in East Sussex.
I've been walking for three hours.

I go up a set of wooden steps that cross over an electric
sheep fence. I've never seen a contraption like this before. I
pass Gap Bottom, which was a point favoured by smugglers,
who in the 18th century would bring ashore their cargoes of
brandy, lace and other contraband. Some met their deaths on
the rocks below. The wreck of the ship *The Cooata* can be
seen at low tide near Flagstaff Point. On the cliffs here is a
monument made from Sarsen Stone. This boulder was left
stranded on top of the chalk when the rocks around it were
eroded some 50 million years ago. Fixed on it is a plaque
commemorating the National Trust's purchase of Crowlink
Valley. Further along, just above the slopes of Michel Dean,
there is another memorial stone. This one is in memory of
W.A. Robertson, whose two brothers were killed at the

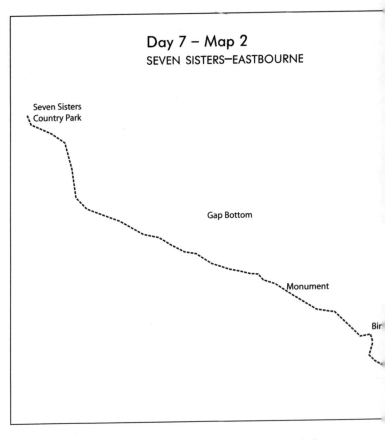

Day 7 – Map 2
SEVEN SISTERS–EASTBOURNE

Seven Sisters
Country Park

Gap Bottom

Monument

Bir

Somme during World War One. Belle Tout, a lighthouse built in the early 19th century and now a private residence, comes up in the distance.

I carry on past cows that don't give me a second look. I bet they haven't seen many people today. I suppose they're thinking, 'What's this nutter doing out in weather like this? He must need his brains testing. He must have mad human's disease.'

At the end of the Seven Sisters is a bridle gate. I go through

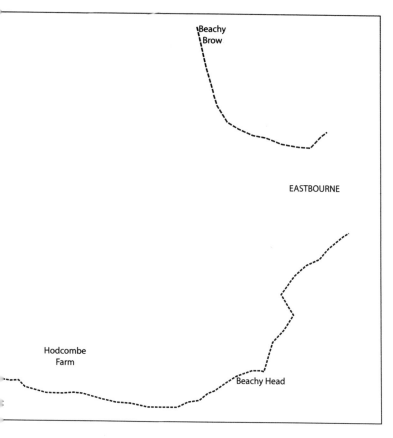

Beachy
Brow

EASTBOURNE

Hodcombe
Farm

Beachy Head

it and turn right and then left. I can see a red phone box next to a row of cottages at the bottom of the hill, and the path goes past some bungalows and into the Birling Gap. There is a car park here with a hotel, restaurant and bar. Fishermen have to winch their boats 30ft up the near-vertical cliff. A mile inland from here is the village of East Dean, once a centre for smugglers; the Tiger Inn there was used as a meeting place because it is situated on a broad triangular green, so it was easy to look out for people approaching.

The South Downs Way runs up the side of the lifeboat building and up some steps towards Lookout Hill, where there is an Iron Age fort. Remember that when Iron and Bronze Age people lived in these parts, the cliffs, before their erosion, would have been up to two miles further out to sea. From Lookout Hill I make my way towards Belle Tout. The walk up to it reminds me of a long fairway on a golf course. Belle Tout looks more like something from a science-fiction film than a lighthouse. The Way runs on the landward side of Belle Tout and goes downhill towards the Beachy Head road. There's a car park here and an information board. Hodcombe Farm, surrounded by stunted trees, is across the other side of the road. It's uphill yet again and my legs are killing me. It's getting dark and a mist is coming in off the sea. At the bottom of Shooter Bottom are three yellow concrete markers. From the top of the hill they look like a brightly coloured aeroplane propeller, but in fact they are used to measure the rates of cliff erosion from aerial photographs.

The red and white candy stripes of Beachy Head Lighthouse, which was repainted in 1995, are just in front of me just half a mile off shore. The beam from the 142ft-high lighthouse can be seen for over 16 miles, and in foggy weather it sounds its foghorn to warn ships away from the perils of the 534ft cliff face at Beachy Head. The lighthouse was originally built in 1902 by steam winching huge stone blocks into position – some sections weighed over five tons. Since 1983 the lighthouse has been operated automatically.

I reach Beachy Head having walked for just over four hours. I pass the rebuilt pub and restaurant. There are toilets here and a bus stop – the service runs into nearby Eastbourne. Just before the pub I stop and have a drink and take off my wet-weather trousers. The octagonal brick shelter I'm sitting on is the base of a 19th-century signalling station. From here messages were sent to the London offices of the Lloyds insurance brokers confirming the safe return of ships and cargoes. At the Battle of Beachy Head in 1690 a combination of English and Dutch boats under the command of the Earl of Torrington engaged the French fleet, just part of the battle to defend these shores from the French hordes and Louis XIV, who if he had been victorious would have appointed the Catholic James Stuart as king, thus placing Britain under the religious leadership and authority of Rome.

The South Downs Way is badly signposted here, so I check my map and am careful not to go off in just any direction. Otherwise I could quite easily get lost and end up having to trek back up some steep track. I pass the path commemorating the United Nations Peace Year and from here on it's guesswork. It's nearly dark and the mist drifting in off the sea is getting thicker.

I head towards the lights of Eastbourne, twinkling away in the semi-darkness, past the playing fields of Whitbread Hole. Here there are football and rugby posts and marked-out pitches, but it still seems quite a distance from civilisation. I pass a wooden hut that must serve as a changing-room. The sound of waves crashing on the rocks down below me sends me slightly inland, where I pick up a track that swings around the edge of the sports field. I follow a wrought-iron fence with the sea down below. Lights come up 200 yards in front of me, and I'm facing a main road. The sound of children playing and laughing fills the cold, dark air as I pass a school. There are cars parked here as well as a bus stop. There's also a small ice-cream kiosk, which is closed, and an information board.

I've somehow managed to reach the start/finish for the South Downs Way! I've done it – I've completed the whole walk. Today's walk has taken me five and a half hours, a lot longer then I anticipated, but it sinks in now that I've cycled from the start over in Carlisle Road, which is the other side of Eastbourne, to Winchester, and now I've walked from Winchester to Eastbourne. It's taken me seven days' walking altogether and many blisters and aching limbs, but I've done it and I've enjoyed it, and, you know what, I fancy doing it again.

I decide to walk along the front and head in the direction of the railway station and the town centre. It's only 5.30 in the evening but the place is deserted. I can see the pier in the distance. A string of lights decorate it, lighting up the winter gloom. The 1,000ft-long pier was designed by Eugenius Birch in 1872, and it was built purely for pleasure. The main attraction to those promenading along the pier was the sensation of walking on the deck of a ship, a sort of poor man's 'don't leave the dock' cruise. It was built on the site of an old Roman villa. In the summer months from here, weather permitting, you can take a boat tour on a 45-minute, seven-mile cruise to Beachy Head. With the retired population of Eastbourne two-and-a-half times the national average, no wonder there's no one on the streets at this unearthly hour. I decide to give the train and bus a miss and take a taxi back to Alfriston.

There are so many memories I'll cherish from my time walking and cycling up on the Downs. There's the scenery, the open rolling countryside, the villages and the friendliness of my fellow walkers and cyclists. But the one thing that will stick in my mind forever is the sight of Martin Knight soaked to the skin with his trousers hanging around his ankles, glasses steamed up, nipping behind a bush after getting caught short.

TOURIST INFORMATION
Eastbourne Tel: 01323 411400

YOUTH HOSTEL
Beachy Head Tel: 01323 721081

TAXIS
Eastbourne and Country Taxis Tel: 01323 720720
Centre Cars, Eastbourne Tel: 01323 508888

BUSES
There's a bus station near the railway station; buses run from
here to Lewes, Alfriston, Brighton, Bexhill, Battle and
Hastings

RAILWAY
Trains run from here along the coast in both directions and
into London

PLACES OF INTEREST
Sovereign Harbour, a new development, just outside
Eastbourne with a marina and waterfront shops, pubs,
restaurants. Try Di Lieto's excellent coffee lounge; the food
and drinks are something else and are real value for money.
The Royal Greenwich Observatory, near Herstmonceux.
The Martello Tower, Eastbourne, a museum which tells the
story of Napoleon's threat to invade England.
Treasure Island, a children's play centre. A great day out for
the kids.
Fort Fun and Rocky's in Eastbourne is a two-acre, family fun
park.

TOWNS AND VILLAGES

CHICHESTER

CHICHESTER IS THE ADMINISTRATIVE capital of West Sussex, with a cathedral that dates back to Norman times. The city is steeped in history: the Romans called it 'Norviomagus' and the simple system of four main streets going north, south, east and west from a central point is still in evidence today. Parts of the circular wall built to protect the city can also still be seen. The largely traffic-free central shopping area around the clock tower and market cross is full of wonderful Georgian houses and shops. Chichester is well known for its Festival Theatre, built in 1962, and it hosts an annual theatre season.

The sea plays a big part in local history and Chichester harbour, with its water tours, is only a short walk or drive out of the city. There are many places of interest nearby: the Roman palace at Fishbourne and the small coastal village of Bosham (pronounced 'bozzam') are well worth a visit, and Goodwood House and racecourse are both nearby as is the military aviation museum at Tangmere and the Royal Military Police museum at the Roussillon barracks, just off the A286.

Chichester is easy to get to with frequent trains from London, or further along the coast from Portsmouth or Brighton. By road Chichester is just off the A27 or A259.

LEWES

THE NAME LEWES COMES from the Anglo-Saxon word 'hlaew', meaning hill, and the Norman priory and castle sit on one of these, looking down over this historic town. The River Ouse cuts through the hills and high chalk faces that straddle the architecture, which ranges from Roman through to modern, and Saxon and Norman to Georgian and Victorian.

The narrow streets known as the 'Twittens' are filled with antique markets and bric-a-brac shops. The Saxons even created a mint to encourage trade to the area and this was continued by the invading Normans who built the town's castle. Throughout the history of the south of England, Lewes has been a strategic trading route. Fish for the local market was bought fresh from the coast along Juggs Road, which is part of the South Downs Way. The Romans connected Lewes with London as one of their main supply routes from the coast into the capital.

Today there are many places of interest and Lewes conveys an air of elegance and sophistication; it has even been called the 'Knightsbridge of the South', and with its cobbled streets and picturesque cottages and galleries, along with the town's colourful heritage, it is clear that the area is not short of wealth and interesting history.

DEW PONDS

THE TERM 'DEW POND' is a recent one. As recently as 100 or 200 years ago they were called 'sheep ponds', 'mist ponds', 'fog ponds' or 'cloud ponds'. These shallow, saucer-shaped ponds were first created by downland sheep farmers before the invention of plastic water piping. There were literally thousands of them along the South Downs Way and their sole purpose was to supply drinking water for sheep and cattle. Even in the hottest summer these watering holes don't seem to dry up. The first dew ponds used as watering holes were natural and caused by cows' hooves trampling an indent into the chalky surface, which then held water. The early artificial ones were lined with clay, with a little quicklime added to stop insect and worm damage. Some ponds had straw added to stop cracking along the pond walls.

In the 20th century a Mr Edward A. Martin was given a grant by the Royal Geographical Society to undertake a series of experiments to discover the true source of the water supply to the dew ponds. The tests lasted more than three years and in that time he concluded that the filling of these ponds had nothing whatsoever to do with dew, mist, fog or supernatural phenomena. It was good old-fashioned rainfall that was refilling these water holes.

Other theories about the origins of dew ponds are that people in the Stone and Iron Ages discovered patches of worn-away chalk or flint that held water just below the clay surface. Most animals will find water if left to their own devices, so people may not have discovered these refreshment fonts after all. Modern-day dew ponds tend to be cast in concrete but you can still see them along the ridges of the Downs. Some, like the ones at Ditchling Beacon and Chanctonbury, are the same as they have been for the last 100 years or so, while others, like those at White Lion and Red Lion ponds near Beddingham Hill, have long dried up.

AMBERLEY

AMBERLEY'S ORIGINS ARE Saxon. In AD 680 the king of the southern Saxons gifted this small Sussex hamlet, as it was then, to the Bishop of Northumbria, who lived at that time at Selsey, near Chichester. The present-day castle at Amberley was originally an undefended house. In 1377 Bishop William Rede got permission to build a wall around his house to create a castle. In 1643, during the English civil war, the castle was badly damaged when Oliver Cromwell sent troops to seize unpaid taxes.

The village and castle changed little until 1863 when the railway was built and new trade routes opened up. This, coupled with an upturn in trade for the local chalk pit and the expansion of lime quarrying, prompted a population boom. In 1872 the castle was sold by the church to Lord Zouche of Parham, who owned it for 21 years before selling it to the Duke of Norfolk, and it is now a private home, and a hotel and restaurant.

The chalk pits are now open to the public as an open-air industrial museum. The village has a few riverside bars, pubs, and restaurants and tea-rooms. Boat hire is also available, so you can enjoy the River Arun or stroll along the banks into nearby Pulborough or to the Black Rabbit pub just outside Arundel.